WORLD POVERTY AND
THE CHRISTIAN

IS VOLUME

132

OF THE

Twentieth Century Encyclopedia of Catholicism

UNDER SECTION

XIII

CATHOLICISM AND SCIENCE

IT IS ALSO THE

102ND

VOLUME IN ORDER OF PUBLICATION

THE TWENTIETH CENTURY ENCYCLOPEDIA · OF CATHOLICISM ·

Edited by **HENRI DANIEL-ROPS** *of the Académie Française*

WORLD POVERTY
AND THE CHRISTIAN

By ARTHUR MC CORMACK

HAWTHORN BOOKS · PUBLISHERS · *New York*

First Edition, March, 1963

NIHIL OBSTAT

Daniel Duivesteijn, S.T.D.

  Censor Deputatus

IMPRIMATUR

Georgius L. Craven

  Episcopus Sebastopolis, Vic. Cap.

Westmonasterii, die II FEBRUARII MCMLXIII

H-9531

CONTENTS

ACKNOWLEDGEMENTS

It is obvious that a writer on such a wide subject as the theme of this book must rely heavily on the work of others. This indebtedness is acknowledged, in part, at least, in the Bibliography and in the footnotes though it is much wider than these would indicate. My special reliance on the work of Fr Drogat, S.J., in Chap. I and of Douglas Hyde and Barbara Ward in Chap. V will be evident to all who know their writings on this subject.

My very sincere thanks go to the typists who made the rapid production of the MS possible, Mrs. D. Critchfield, Miss Alice Reardon and Miss L. McCormack, my sister. I owe special gratitude to Mr. and Mrs. A. Mahon of Ealing for their hospitality during the whole writing of this book.

ARTHUR McCORMACK

CHAPTER I

THE EXTENT OF WORLD POVERTY

RICH COUNTRIES AND POOR COUNTRIES

The central fact of the second half of the twentieth century is the existence of world poverty and under-development.

The world is divided into two groups of people: the "haves" and the "have nots"; those who live in plenty and those who stagnate in want and are familiar only with the fear of hunger, of sickness and of death. As Dr B. R. Sen, Director General of the F.A.O., has said: "One does not have to seek the aid of statistics to discover the widespread poverty that exists in many parts of the world today. It is visible to the naked eye; one merely has to walk in these parts of the world with one's eyes open."

Poverty and under-development are easy to recognize, but not so easy to define. Nevertheless, some attempt must be made to give a statistical framework to the picture of a world in want in order to bring home the extent of the problem. Various experts use different methods to estimate this. They all agree on the *fact* of world need.

One hundred great communities of the world are dreadfully poor, according to Paul Hoffman, who, as head of the United Nations Special Fund, is in a position to know. The annual income per person of the 1,250 million people in these countries is slightly over 100 dollars or roughly £35. In other words, reckoning the population of the world at 3,000 million, well over one-third of the world's inhabitants have only about 15*s.* or just over 2 dollars per week on which to live. In many countries, the *per capita* income is still lower; as low as £20 or 57 dollars per person, for example, in India with its 438 million inhabitants.

Pierre Moussa has fixed the threshold of poverty at a higher level, at approximately 200 dollars or £70 per head per annum. On this basis, the poor areas of the world would include Asia, excluding the U.S.S.R., Japan and Israel, making 1,400 million people; part of Eastern Europe and certain peripheral countries of Western Europe, making in all about 100 million Europeans; all of Africa except the Union of South Africa, or 200 million Africans; continental and insular Latin America, except the countries in the southern tip of South America, making upward of 150 million Latin Americans; finally nearly all Oceania, less Australia and New Zealand, adding a further few million. On this basis, the under-developed part of the world contains between 1,850 and 1,900 thousand million people, or nearly two-thirds of the human race.

Of course, this way of measuring poverty does not give a completely clear picture. Statistics do not tell the whole truth. There are prosperous enclaves in this map of under-development. Within a country there will be many who have much more than the average and many who sink below even the low normal figure.

For example, as President Betancourt has pointed out, in a country like Venezuela, which has the highest *per capita* income on paper of the South American States, hundreds of thousands of families are wretchedly poor. The reason is that the huge income from the oil wells increases the total national income enormously and therefore increases the *per capita* income (obtained by dividing the total income by the number of inhabitants), but the oil revenues do not find their way into the pockets of the poor.

There is the additional difficulty that income expressed in money is an inadequate guide to real wealth or poverty, as the cost of living must also be taken into account. What economists call real income, that is, the amount of goods or services money can buy, is obviously important, especially in comparing standards of living in different countries. Nevertheless, with the need and desire of developing countries to have the goods of the developed countries, this distinction is not of so much practical importance as hitherto. To take a very simple example: for an Indian to buy a bicycle which may be useful or even necessary for him would take almost the whole of his income for one year. Or another more important illustration: economists reckon that to achieve healthy economic growth, developing countries need to save between 10 per cent and 15 per cent of their income. Ten per cent of £20 is not very much, yet it represents a huge amount to those whose income is so low.

Comparison of *per capita* incomes, therefore, although a rough yardstick, is probably the best we have got and does highlight the gap between those who want for nothing and those who lack almost everything. Although the developing countries, in spite of the population expansion, have in some ways bettered their position in the last twenty years, the gap is growing wider for a number of reasons, mainly because wealth begets wealth and poverty breeds poverty in a vicious circle, so well described by Gunnar Myrdal and others.

The people of the United States now have an annual *per capita* income of 2,800 dollars or nearly £1,000. In 1938, the average *per capita* income in the United States was fifteen times greater than in India. Today, in spite of the great leap forward that India has made through the first two Five Year Plans, the difference is thirty-five times as great.

A comparison of national incomes gives a picture of the distribution of wealth throughout the world and shows that the greater part of mankind is, relatively, very poor. The Far East, with 52·3 per cent of the total world population, has only 12·3 per cent of the world income. Africa, with 7·1 per cent of the population, has 2·2 per cent of that income. Latin America has 6·8 per cent of the population, but only 4·7 per cent of the total income. On the other hand, Oceania, with only 0·5 per cent of the total population, has 1·5 per cent of the total income. North America and Europe, of course, are the wealthiest—North America, with 6·7 per cent of the population, has 39·8 per cent of the income, and Europe, with 22·2 per cent of the population, has 37·7 per cent of the income.

The nineteen richest countries in the world, representing only 16 per cent of its population, control three-quarters of the world's income. Eleven per cent of the cereals, 75 per cent of the fats, 64 per cent of the sugar consumed by the affluent countries come to them from the poorer half of the world.

THE EFFECTS OF POVERTY

Countries with a low *per capita* income are called under-developed countries, or, more hopefully, developing countries. From an economic point of view, an under-developed country is essentially one with a very low standard of living, insufficient progress in well-being and conditions unfavourable to development.

In human terms, this means that many of the peoples in these countries are poor, hungry, subject to disease, living in conditions unworthy of human beings, illiterate and under-employed. In presenting our statistics it must never be forgotten that this is a human problem, concerning human beings: the people who live in a million villages where there is no leeway for misfortune and where despair constantly vies with hope, and those who live in slums, well below what most of us in the West would regard as the extreme limit of imaginable poverty.

Hunger

Hunger is the concomitant of poverty. It stalks the world today. Sometimes it does so dramatically when famine strikes or when the horrors of war throw up a spate of refugees threatened with starvation. But millions of people do not get enough to eat in normal times. Under-nourishment is endemic in under-developed countries. It is true that sometimes the amount of actual hunger has been exaggerated. It does not seem to be a fact that two out of three people go to bed hungry. But the best sources—the 1957 and 1961 Reports of the F.A.O.—suggest that about one-seventh of the world's population, between 300–450 million, are underfed. The 1961 F.A.O. report estimated that those suffering from the concealed hunger of malnutrition, the cause of deficiency diseases such as kwashiorkor, pellagra, beri-beri, and keratomalacia, number nearly half the inhabitants of the world.

It is hard to assess the actual amount of hunger on the rough basis of calorie and protein intake for there are a number of variables (such as climate, body weight, kind of work, etc.) to be taken into account, and it is therefore difficult to define hunger in these terms, but a rough guide can be obtained by comparing the amount of calorie intake in developed countries with that of the under-developed. In Britain during the war, it was found that below an average of 2,800 calories there was loss of weight suggesting an inadequate diet.

Bearing this figure in mind, let us examine present world calorie levels. On the basis of available figures, it appears that food supplies of countries representing only about 20 per cent or one-fifth of the world's population exceed a calorie level of 2,800. On the other hand, the food supplies of countries representing no less than 60 per cent of the world's population actually fall below 2,200 of which nearly half are below 2,000— a figure 800 calories less than that at which British adults and children started to lose weight. And, of course, these are average figures; many will be below this.

Moreover, it is the tropical and sub-tropical lands which are mainly affected. All twenty-one countries which exceed the 2,800 calorie level are located in either Europe, North America, Oceania (that is, Australia and New Zealand) or the River Plate area. Of the fifty remaining countries for which figures are available, only eight are located in Europe; the remainder are in the under-developed regions of the Near East, the Far East, Latin America and the tropical parts of Africa. The level of nutrition in the Far East is among the lowest known.

The individual intake of calories in south-east Asia is not even as much as two-thirds of that in the more developed countries of Europe. In India, the typical intake is less than half that in Australia, New Zealand, Argentina and the United States. This situation is highlighted by a passage quoted by Tibor Mende:

> One hundred million villagers have never had enough to eat. Investigators will tell you that the Indian people are under-nourished. But that has been their condition for ten or twenty generations, since long before there were any investigators. The Indian's bone formation and his very shape have been modified, thinned and made weaker. Hence the disquieting grace of these slim figures with breadth neither of shoulders nor of hips. One would swear that the enormous eyes, admirable in themselves, have eaten up their faces.

Fully to study the subject, one should examine the map of hunger, country by country, as Noël Drogat, S.J., in his *Challenge of Hunger*, and others have done.

But this impressionistic sketch—all there is space for—is enough to show the gap between the nutritional standards of the prosperous countries and the less fortunate areas of the world and to prove that quite literally millions, hundreds of millions, do not get enough to eat.

Comparison of typical diets pinpoints another difference. For example, comparison between a typical urban diet in the United States and a typical diet of a rice-eating working-class family in India shows how widely nutritional standards vary. The Indian consumes 1·23 pounds of food a day, the American city dweller 4·66 pounds. Rice, the basis of the Indian diet, represents 85 per cent of the daily food. Lacking an adequate supply of proteins, fats and vitamins, the Indian worker is subject to many diseases due to malnutrition, is lowered in stamina and has a shorter life expectancy. This condition reduces his energy and ability to work and thus to contribute in full to the economic development of his country.

The American diet is remarkable for its diversity and is one of the best balanced. It has resulted in building a strong and healthy people who have achieved the most remarkable economic development in the Western Hemisphere.

This comparison brings in two factors we have not yet considered: the effects of hunger and the dearth of protein and other ingredients of a balanced diet.

Under-nourishment not only has a physical effect on the body, shown in reduction of weight and reduction in physical activity, but it also causes behaviour symptoms such as lack of mental alertness and creative thinking, apathy, depression and irritability—leading in extreme cases to increasing loss of moral standards and social ties. The evidence of observers in famine conditions bears witness to the accuracy of the final statement: even cannibalism has been known in the famines that have been the scourge of China and India and the Far East generally, in past generations, and even in this.

Disease

Under-nutrition is, of course, also linked with low resistance to diseases such as tuberculosis. It is a major cause of the inability and lack of inclination to work. When Gandhi blamed the indolence of the Indian peasant for the poverty of his country, he was less than fair to its inhabitants, because he did not consider the underlying causes of this. There is no reason to suppose that this is the natural and inevitable trait of people in tropical countries, when it may be due largely to the fact that they are not as well fed and as healthy as people in wealthy countries. These considerations also give point to the remark of an Indian to a European: "For us Asiatics the most important thing is not to be free, but to eat regularly".

Recently, Mr Sen Gupta of the Indian High Commissioner's office in London said that even now 20 per cent of India's population, that is over 80 million people, do not get enough to eat. It is no wonder the saintly Gandhi said: "To the millions who have to go without two meals a day the only acceptable form in which God dare appear is food." Mr Sen Gupta also said that nearly the whole population suffered from the concealed hunger of malnutrition, the lack of adequate protein and other ingredients of a balanced diet.

I have dealt so far mainly with under-nutrition, namely with inadequacies in the total supplies of food. But in most under-developed countries there are inadequacies not only in the quantity of food, but in its quality—leading to malnutrition as well as to under-nutrition. In the developed countries the diet is commonly drawn from a wide variety of sources, and the staple cereals and starchy roots do not constitute an ab-normally high proportion of the total food intake. The reverse is true of the under-developed countries. Thus, whereas the proportion of staple cereals and starchy roots in the North American diet is estimated to be only 25 per cent, and in the British diet only 31 per cent, in Europe as a whole it is 50 per cent, in Latin America 54, in Africa 66, in the Near East 71 and in the Far East over 73 per cent. Conversely, while the proportion of animal products—milk, meat, eggs and fish—in the North American diet reaches the exceptionally high figure of 40 per cent and in the British diet as high as 27 per cent, the figure for Europe as a whole is estimated at 21 per cent, for Latin America 17, for Africa 11, for the Near East 9, and for the Far East 5 per cent. These differences are reflected in the shortage of protein, and particularly of animal protein, in the diets of the under-developed countries, the figures for total protein (expressed in grams per head per day) falling from 92 in North America to 57 in the Far East, and for animal protein falling still more strikingly from 66 in North America to only 7 in the Far East—a tenfold difference.[1] Simultaneously, owing to the lack of variety in the diets of the less-developed countries and particularly to the shortage of animal products, such diets also tend to lack adequate quantities of vitamins and essential mineral constituents. This in turn leads to the incidence of specific deficiency diseases—diseases which are seldom encountered in the more developed countries.

[1] *Animal protein*: Far East—8 grams per day; Near East—14 grams per day; Latin America—24 grams per day; Europe—38 grams per day; North America—66 grams per day.

Of these diseases, probably the most widespread in its incidence and the most damaging in its effects is that now known—from its original African name—as *kwashiorkor*. This condition is found most frequently in children between weaning and about four to six years of age, that is, during the first few years after the child is transferred from a milk diet to a diet which, in under-developed countries, is likely to consist largely of cereals. During this period the protein requirements for growth are high; at the same time the child is particularly vulnerable to various infections which themselves tend to precipitate kwashiorkor. The typical symptoms of the acute condition are edema, wasting and skin sores, accompanied by liver degeneration; unless promptly treated by the administration of supplementary protein, the child usually dies.

Acute cases of this nature form, however, only a small part of the total problem of protein deficiency in children. Less acute cases are widely prevalent, and may result not only in lasting though concealed damage, particularly to the liver, but they frequently exacerbate the effects of intermittent infections, such as measles or dysentery, with a resulting high mortality rate not found among better-fed populations. Indeed, while the prevalence of kwashiorkor itself has been compared with the visible portion of an iceberg, which has six-sevenths concealed beneath the surface, recent studies indicate that its relationship with what has for convenience been termed "pre-kwashiorkor" is rather that of an underseas mountain with only the tip of its peak protruding above the surface. As an illustration of the widespread incidence of this condition it has been claimed that there is probably no African child who has not suffered from such a deficiency at some period of its life, while there is accumulating evidence that the condition is also prevalent in many parts of Central and Latin America and in Asia and the Far East—indeed in all those areas where food supply data indicate a shortage of animal protein.

Kwashiorkor and its less acute companion, pre-kwashiorkor, are moreover by no means the only prevalent deficiency diseases attributable to malnutrition in under-developed countries.

Avitaminosis A is a frequent cause of deficiency symptoms, notably of blindness associated with keratomalacia. Indeed, in many Eastern countries keratomalacia is stated to be at least as potent as smallpox and venereal diseases in destroying children's sight. Avitaminosis A is still prevalent in certain areas of Africa, of Asia and of Latin America. Pellagra is still endemic among populations subsisting largely on a maize diet; it is found in areas of Africa and the Near East and, sporadically, in Latin America. Rickets, normally rare in tropical countries, exists nevertheless in Africa, in parts of Asia and in the Near East. Finally nutritional anaemia, associated with iron deficiency, still constitutes a serious health hazard, especially among expectant mothers and young children, and is the principal factor affecting maternal mortality in a number of under-developed countries.[2]

Relatively few areas of the world, then, are free from want. Throughout large regions in Asia, Africa and Latin America numbers of people suffer from lack of food adequate in quality and quantity to sustain their health, growth and physical vigour. It is no wonder that this has been called the biggest human problem of the century. It is an explosive problem also when it is realized that this is a state of affairs which is no longer accepted as necessary or inevitable. As I. W. Mooman has said: "Nor will peace come to the earth until mass poverty is lifted and the millions who scratch the soil for a precarious living can look up and plough with hope."

This kind of poverty and hunger has no relation to the Christian ideal of voluntary poverty, the detachment from overmuch concern for the riches of life. Religious vows, it is true, bind dedicated souls to the ideal of evangelical poverty, but this is far removed in spirit and fact from degrading poverty, destitution and hunger, of which the pagan Seneca said nearly 2,000 years ago: "A hungry people will not endure reason; they will not listen to justice; they will not even pray."

[2] See *Hunger. Can It Be Averted?* British Association, London, August 1961.

The hunger in the world is not due, as we shall see, to lack of nature's bounty or man's ingenuity. Indeed, in 1958–9, agricultural production in the world, as a whole, was twice as great as even the rapid growth of population, and in a number of countries this relationship was even more favourable in terms of food production. On the other hand, statistics also show that Latin America, the Far East and the Near East have between them three-fifths of the world's population, but they dispose of only one-third of the world's agricultural production and are hardly keeping pace with the rise in their population; indeed, food production in some areas is lagging behind.

Today, in fact, there is more food in the world than ever before, but most men do not eat better. In some cases they are worse off than before World War II.

Bad living conditions

Half the world then is suffering from undernourishment and malnutrition. It is true that only 30 million (only!) actually die of starvation and undernourishment per year. But not to be dying of starvation is surely not the ideal of human life. Hunger is only one of the evils summed up by the unemotional word, under-development. The misery and degradation of poverty include many more human problems: lack of medical services, of basic education, of adequate housing and clothing, the inability to put into practice the simple rules of hygiene which would be a defence against mass diseases, industrial under-development, lack of employment or concealed unemployment, lack of capital and savings to break through the vicious circle of poverty breeding poverty and turn it into a constructive spiral leading to self-sustained growth, lack of opportunities for improvement, even absence of desire to improve caused by years of malnutrition and disease bringing in their train apathy and fatalism.

A few more statistics, helped by our imagination, may give an idea of the huge sum of human misery which world poverty entails. With regard to health services, in the developed countries there is one doctor for every 1,000 inhabitants. In the poor countries, there is one doctor for every 10,000, 50,000 or even 70,000 inhabitants. France alone has more hospital beds than the whole of Asia.

Here I can speak feelingly and may, I hope, be forgiven a reference to personal experience. In the African country where I was for nearly ten years, there were only five doctors in an area nearly the size of England, yet there was far more illness and disease, for tropical ailments were added to ordinary ills. Since returning some years ago from my missionary work, I myself have had nearly two years in hospitals and have had six or seven years of semi-invalidism as a result of my stay in that country. In one mission station where I was, it was two days' walk to the nearest doctor and it took a day for him to come if he was available (in the dry season; it was impossible for him to come in the rainy season). The priest who came after me died in his prime of an ordinary case of pneumonia as a result of these conditions. I had malaria nearly fifty times, but never once the assistance of a doctor. Yet I was a priest and a privileged white man. Unless an African was really near one of the five hospitals, his chance of medical attention and relief from pain was scant indeed, though we missionaries did our best with the resources of medicine and time at our disposal.

In the poorer countries of the world, malaria alone attacks 300 million people every year, 3 million of them fatally; tuberculosis 50 million, 5 million of them fatally; leprosy about 10 million; yaws, trachoma, bilharzia, tens of millions. Apart from the huge amount of human suffering, this represents an economic loss and Dr Pierre Theil has pointed out: "Even to this day, 200 million people in India suffer from malaria. Many of them can do little more than vegetate. To provide treatment for these invalids is to do more than a work of humanity; it is also to furnish the community with producers, where formerly there were only consumers."

The statistics of infant mortality are also revealing. There are huge differences between statistics for developed countries and the under-developed, even between the mortality rates within various classes.

For a great number of these countries we possess only fragmentary statistics. Some interesting results have been obtained in Africa from inquiries set on foot by O.R.A.N.A.[3] Death rates vary between 102 and 340 per thousand in children under one year; 63 to 130 per thousand in children between one year and two; from 298 to 419 per thousand in all children under the age of fourteen years. It is also pointed out by Dr Tremolières that in the great part of the population in the under-developed zones of Upper Volta, inquiries show a sudden check to growth in weight and height appearing at around six months, becoming accentuated between ten and fifteen years of age, and then diminishing and disappearing in adolescence.

In Latin America infantile mortality rates are high, but we do not have figures such as those collected in certain parts of Africa and Asia. In those parts, almost half the children die before they reach the age of five. The United Nations' demographic service has made some estimates of infant mortality for the period 1950–5.[4]

Annual infant mortality rate per thousand live births (approximate)

AMERICA	
Cuba, Mexico, Paraguay	125
Bolivia, Brazil, Colombia, Ecuador, Honduras, Nicaragua, Panama, Peru, Dominican Republic, Venezuela	150
Guatemala, Salvador	175

ASIA	
China (Taiwan)	100
Thailand	175
India, Pakistan, Philippines	200
Burma	225

The rates of infantile mortality shown by these figures may be more than four times those of Western countries. In the countries of Western Europe, Australia and North America

[3] Organisme de Recherches sur l'Alimentation et la Nutrition en Afrique. The headquarters is in Dakar.

[4] U.N. Report on the State of Social Affairs in the World, p. 21 (1957).

the figure is less than 50 per thousand, while it is usually higher than 150 per thousand in the greater part of Asia or even of Latin America. An infant in New Zealand, able to have a diet which is particularly rich in protein, has five times as much chance of surviving his first year than has an Indian or African child.[5]

So, for example, in the Union of South Africa, infant mortality runs at the rate of:

132 per 1,000 among the population of Negro origin
68 per 1,000 among the population of Asiatic origin
28 per 1,000 among the population of White origin.

In practice this means that every black infant born at Cape Town or Pretoria runs five times the risk of dying before reaching the age of one year compared with any white child born in the same towns.

Low expectation of life in under-developed countries is a measure of high infant mortality and a reflection of the lack of adequate medical care. In Egypt, at birth, expectation of life is thirty-five years; in India thirty-two years; in France sixty-three years; in Britain sixty-eight years.

In the Union of South Africa, a new-born Negro even today has an expectation of life of only forty-three years and a new born Asiatic of fifty years, whereas the expectation of life of a new-born white is sixty-six years.

Why? Because the living conditions of Negroes in that country are infinitely more wretched than those of Asiatics, which in turn are already very much inferior to those of the whites.

This phenomenon is met again in Southern Rhodesia, where infant mortality occurs at the rate of:

259 per 1,000 among the indigenous population
81 per 1,000 among the European population

and also in Algeria, where it occurs at the rate of:

108 per 1,000 among the Muslim population, as against
41 per 1,000 among the European population.

[5] Noël Drogat, *The Challenge of Hunger*, Burns and Oates, 1962, pp. 49–50.

Millions of human beings live in conditions which vary from the bad to the appalling. It is no exaggeration to say that many animals in rich countries are treated better. According to approximate estimates (it is impossible to secure accurate data in this field) the number of families living in sub-human conditions totals 150 million in the under-developed countries and 30 million in the countries called prosperous. This means that hundreds of millions of children are growing up in conditions which menace not only their physical development but also their spiritual welfare, exposed as they are to the dangers of vagabondage, prostitution, alcoholism, delinquency, promiscuity, etc.

Pius XII, in his Christmas message of 1952, described the state of such families and made a stirring appeal for drastic and far-reaching reform of economic and social conditions for the sake of the family. Everywhere one finds, he said, families over whom hangs the spectre of hunger, sudden unemployment, of a total loss of means of livelihood, of sudden changes in wages. Many families find that the wages earned are insufficient to buy even the essentials of decent food and clothing, and they are forced to live completely deprived of the simple comforts of life. He goes on:

> But the most desolate picture is presented by families who have simply nothing. These are families in utter wretchedness; the father without work, the mother watching her children waste away, quite powerless to help them; no food for them, never enough clothes to cover them, and woe to the whole family when sickness makes its dread visitation to the cave now become a dwelling place for human beings. . . . Not only do whole generations lose physical hardness but, worse still, they fall into crime and wretched moral depravity.

The slums of South America described, for example, by Raymond Scheyven, prove that this moving picture of human misery is no exaggeration. At Lima, in Peru, almost one-third of the population live in cities of planks and sheet iron which are called the "Barruadas". There is one water tap for one hundred families, while in the centre of the city the golf course is so carefully watered that it is like a good course in England. The same is true of Rio de Janeiro. Slums of about 70,000 each surround the city. These "Favelles" house a third of the population. At Caracas, in Venezuela, they are called "Barrios", and 400,000 people live there. Their plight is truly miserable, bearing out the pope's words about spiritual disasters and moral depravity. They seem to be abandoned by everyone: without priests, without doctors to help them, they give themselves into the hands of witch doctors. The law of the jungle holds sway.

Conditions such as these can be found everywhere in the under-developed world, varying, it is true, in severity but constituting a problem of great magnitude.

Ignorance is the ally of poverty and hunger. Mgr Ligutti, the Vatican Permanent Observer at the F.A.O., told me of a scene he had witnessed in Panama. On one side of the road there was miserable farmland, where poverty-stricken peasants eked out a wretched living with great labour. On the other side, Japanese immigrants had beautiful flourishing farms like market gardens and were rich and prosperous from the same soil, due to their use of modern techniques and "know-how", the fruits of education.

Illiteracy

Illiteracy is the scourge of the under-developed continents. To produce more food and combat the other ills of under-development education at all levels is essential, if these people are to help themselves. The accumulated knowledge and wisdom of mankind, even the ability to read simple instructions, are denied to the illiterate. The way to a good life, to a reasonable standard of living, to a chance to escape from the net of fear and superstition, runs through knowledge.

Yet nearly half (45 per cent) of the children of the world— the poorer half of it mainly—have no chance of education. Much more than half of the people above the age of ten have never been to school. Peru has 52 per cent illiterates, Brazil 51 per cent, Africa as a whole 80 per cent, India 83.4 per cent.

These figures taken at random illustrate the intellectual poverty of the poor of the world. Yet there is a great eagerness to learn and a great ability to profit by learning. Children are prepared to walk miles to school and to work at their studies with great earnestness. I remember a boy walking 250 miles from his "bush" village in West Africa to the only college in his country, of which I was principal and which a few priests and African teachers ran "on a shoestring", with an old zinc-roofed building as our main classroom block. Nineteen years later he was elected a Fellow of the Royal College of Surgeons in London and is now in an important medical post in his own country.

Much has been done and is being done but much more help in money, in teachers and in equipment, is necessary to win the war against ignorance.

Such is the poverty of the under-developed world.

REASONS FOR THE POVERTY OF THE UNDER-DEVELOPED COUNTRIES

Of course, man is adaptable and, in many parts of the world where poverty is not too acute, people can be contented and live apparently happy lives in conditions which would spell misery for Europeans. Some of the inhabitants of the country where I worked were much happier than well-off people in England, proving that man does not live by bread alone. It is sometimes said, too, as it was said about the industrial workers of Victorian England, that they know no better and that we should leave them in their state of apathetic content instead of trying to improve their lot. I have even heard it said that we had to work hard to get our prosperity, so let them work hard to get theirs. Such specious reasoning does not stand up to the lessons of history or the present realities. As Mr Nehru said, it is not poverty and misery which are new; the new thing is that people are now conscious of their plight and are determined to emerge from it.

Still, it may be useful to sketch briefly the reasons why the world is divided into the "haves" and the "have nots": what are the causes of world poverty, why is this one half of the world so dreadfully poor? Or perhaps the question should be phrased differently. Why is it that the West has emerged from the poverty and ignorance which has been the lot of large numbers of mankind since the world began?

The most obvious reason is the scientific and industrial revolution. This revolution began in the eighteenth century, with its roots in medieval scientific thought and the humanist culture of the Renaissance, and has been gathering momentum in Western civilization ever since.

The mastery of nature by means of the machine has put at man's disposal sources of energy and power which have enabled him to multiply the power of his hands and brain. For example, a primitive farmer can support five or six people working with his hands and rudimentary tools. A Canadian farmer, by means of mechanized aids to agriculture, can grow food for 470 people. The use of coal, the invention of steel, of the steam engine, of electrical power have harnessed the forces of nature to bring the riches and advantages of modern civilization to the West.

The discoveries of medicine and the spread of universal education have brought with them cumulative benefits which have increased the well-being of Western man. The inventiveness and capacity for work which have developed in temperate climates have, for several centuries, been spurred on by a desire for increased productivity, itself geared to economic competition. These traits may indeed owe something to the climate of the more temperate lands, but they probably owe as much to the attitude to material prosperity and progress which developed when the Wars of Religion were drifting to their inevitable stalemate. The value of work as a means of developing the present world in which we live, the religious idea that it was good to labour but wrong to squander the fruits of labour, produced a favourable climate in which capitalism, or at least the accumulation of capital to be ploughed back into further development and progress, could flourish. This attitude in its turn was due to revolt from the over-emphasis on other-worldly values to be found in medieval civilization and which are even more evident in the culture and way of life of much of the East.

These developments have taken place roughly in the last 300 years. It is probable that the standard of living of an English or French peasant differed little from that of the Egyptian in 1650. In a few generations the difference between the West and the rest of the world has reached extraordinary proportions. In the nineteenth century, the riches of the Western countries were a glaring contrast to the poverty of the rest of the world, though inside these countries there was great poverty and economic oppression. In the twentieth century, poverty has largely been wiped out within the Western nations and the mass of the population in Western countries enjoys a standard of living undreamt of except by the very rich in bygone centuries.

The rest of the world did not profit to the same extent from the inventiveness and wealth of the Europeans and the inhabitants of North America, which was peopled by emigrants from Europe.

The colonizing powers on the whole, especially in the eighteenth and nineteenth centuries, were concerned with their own trade, their own prosperity, and regarded overseas territories as the source of trading goods or raw materials. They were gradually forced to extend their rule, to found empires almost in spite of themselves. In doing so, they brought benefits of law and order and a certain amount of beneficial social change—one thinks of India in the nineteenth century for example—but there was little realization of the plight of the ordinary people, sunk in the poverty of centuries, and little awareness or hope on the part of these peoples that their life could be any different from what they had always been used to.

The revulsion from colonialism has probably caused its evils to be over-emphasized and its benefits to be minimized. Events in Africa and elsewhere have stressed that law and order are no mean boons: in fact they are the essentials of civilized life and the pre-conditions for any progress. Especially since

World War II, more enlightened colonial policies have brought great benefits to developing countries and made possible their emergence as independent countries, prematurely perhaps, in certain cases. A comparison of the progress and prosperity of some West African British or French colonies with Liberia under non-colonial rule, or of India or the Dutch East Indies with neighbouring states which were not colonies might temper the harsh strictures on colonialism which are fashionable to-day. Nevertheless, until recently, the main aims of the colonizing powers were self-regarding and led to a sporadic and uneven development of the colonies' economy with an unbalanced dependence on primary products and raw materials of benefit to the mother country.

But this century, especially since the war, has witnessed an awakening of such magnitude as to justify Adlai Stevenson's phrase the "revolution of rising expectations". Since the war, nearly 1,000 million people have gained their independence. They have not done so in order to starve but to win for themselves lives free from the degradation of poverty and worthy of their dignity as human beings. This is not, of course, the conscious motivation of many of these millions nor is it always the single-minded aim of the political leaders who have won their freedom, but it is quite certain that they do not intend to acquiesce in the glaring inequalities which are evident in the world today. The fires of envy have been lit. In some they may burn as a resentful covetousness, but for many they light up a praiseworthy desire to win for themselves and their people a share of the prosperity that their former masters so obviously have.

Side by side with this awakening has come the realization to the more prosperous countries that justice, charity and prudence impel them to share their riches with the peoples of whose poverty they are becoming really aware for the first time. This awareness has been with far-sighted statesmen for some time, indeed since the end of World War II. Pius XII on many occasions strove to arouse and strengthen it. It was behind the founding of the F.A.O., the Four Freedoms of the United

Nations Charter, it was the inspiration of Marshall Aid, and it has increased during the past decade to such an extent that it is beginning to reach the ordinary people in the Western democracies. With it has come the feeling that poverty is an anachronism in the twentieth century, when we have all the technical know-how and resources for the first time in human history to wipe poverty off the face of the earth.

CHAPTER II

THE POPULATION EXPANSION AND WORLD POVERTY

THE INCREASE IN WORLD POPULATION

In the past decade, and especially in the last three or four years, increasing attention has been focused on the population expansion of the twentieth century, often called "the population explosion", which many regard as the central problem of our age.

And, indeed, this century has witnessed a growth in world population without parallel in history. This rapid increase in the number of people inhabiting our limited earth and in the rate of this increase is expected to continue, at least for some time.

Numerically speaking, then, mankind is much larger, is growing more rapidly and faces prospects of even greater growth than ever before.

At the beginning of the century, the population of the world was 1,602 million. At present (May 1962) it has just reached the 3,000 million mark, and the well-founded estimates of the United Nations Population Commission give about six billion—possibly more—by the end of the century.

The population of the world is increasing at the rate of 1·8 per cent per year. In other words every year there are 54 million more people, every day there are 170,000 more mouths to be fed, every second there are two more people added to the human sum.

All the above countries enjoy a high standard of living. (These may be compared with India with a population density of 308 per sq. mile.)

Examples of sparsely populated countries:

Country	Rate of increase %	Population per sq. mile	Country	Rate of increase %	Population per sq. mile
Cameroons	0·6	17	Congo (Brazzaville)	—	5
Congo (Leopoldville)	2·2	15	Ghana	1·6	52
Nigeria	1·9	95	Senegal	3.6	32
Tunisia	1·4	77	Kenya	1·6	27
Uganda	2·5	67	Tanganyika	1·8	25
Canada	2·7	5	Argentina	1·9	17
Bolivia	1·4	7	Brazil	2·4	20
Chile	2·5	25	Ecuador	3·0	37
Paraguay	2·3	10	Peru	2·6	20
Venezuela	3·0	17	Indonesia	2·1	152
North Borneo	2·8	15	Sarawak	2·5	12

Examples of comparatively heavily populated countries:

Country	Rate of increase %	Population per sq. mile	Country	Rate of increase %	Population per sq. mile
Mauritius	3·1	832	Costa Rica	4·1	55
Guatemala	3·0	85	United States of America	1·7	47
West Indies	2·2	387			
Jamaica	2·0	365	Barbados	1·3	1382
Puerto Rico	1·0	660	Trinidad and Tobago	3·2	397
China (Mainland)	2·8	175	Ceylon	2·5	367
Philippines	2·6	205	India	1·3	307
Portugal	0·8	245	Italy	0·5	407
Malta and Gozo	0·4	2570	Spain	0·8	147

Source: U.N. Demographic Yearbook 1960 (U.N., New York, 1961).

There have been and are a number of advantages in a large and expanding population. This was experienced in England and other industrial countries in the nineteenth century. The infra-structures of a country's economy, roads, railways, public services and so on, are only really worth while and only get adequate fiscal support with a large number of people. A large number of potential consumers helps the development of industries and supplies, at the same time, a large market for the goods produced and even helps to correct investment errors.

However, the poorer countries of the world subject to population pressure are not so happily off as the European countries were in the eighteenth or nineteenth century. Industrial progress had begun before population increase and was able to absorb greatly increased manpower and there were large open lands to siphon off any excess.

The plight of the under-developed countries today from a population point of view is far different and more serious. They are mostly economically backward. They are faced with the need to provide the pre-conditions for what Rostow has called "take-off" into self-sustaining economic growth which needs investment, in other words, savings from inadequate incomes of the region of 10 per cent to 15 per cent of annual income. But demographic investment also increases with increasing population. By demographic investment I mean all the services which are needed to cope with population growth, more schools, houses, medical services, etc.

Poor countries with population doubling in thirty, forty or fifty years—and an increase rate of 2 per cent means a doubling in fifty years—have a big strain on their developing economies. This tends to swallow up progress and savings merely in keeping up with increasing population.

India is a good example of this. Throughout most of the decade of the first two Five Year Plans, which began in 1951, her population increase was less than that of most developing countries, much less than 2 per cent in fact. But the annual increase of five million per year rising to eight million towards the end of the period on a population which had risen to 402,600 million (with a density of nearly 300 per square mile) by 1959, combined with the comparatively slow rate of economic growth led to a certain amount of overall stagnation with its attendant miseries, in spite of increased economic progress and generous aid from abroad. In the next fifteen or twenty years, far from an expanding population increasing an expanding economy, the projected population growth (for example, it is expected to be 460 millions by 1965) will bring no marked advantage, since the increase will be mainly in the under-fifteen-years group. Whereas a rapidly growing population, given room for expansion, has economic and psychological advantages in the long run, short-term prospects show that a slower rate of growth would increase per-consumer income— by as much as 60 per cent according to Coale and Hoover— if, instead of the present rate of increase, fertility were to be reduced.

However, to reduce fertility significantly by any means of family planning available at present would, even in the view of those most keen to propagate contraception, take a generation. Consequently, widespread family planning would be reducing fertility just when from an economic point of view such a reduction was no longer necessary or even desirable. If long-term economic plans develop as they should, the country will be on an economic upsurge and will be able to absorb or even need an increasing population to keep up this impetus.

MORAL REASONS FOR THE CHURCH'S OPPOSITION TO CONTRACEPTION

In a book appearing in a series like the present, it seems appropriate that the full reasons for the Catholic opposition to artificial birth control to reduce the "menace" of numbers should be clearly stated. Many have regarded the Church's attitude as old-fashioned, unprogressive, unrealistic, doctrinaire and even inhumane as refusing to poverty-stricken, rapidly expanding peoples the panacea for their plight. Population restriction by means of contraceptive techniques is already widely available and effective in the developed countries. Even those who do not accept the dilemma, "birth control or starvation", or share the extreme views of the doctrinaire family planners, feel that the Church is blocking one promising way of helping the under-developed countries. They especially resent the Church's attitude in international bodies where there is pressure from some countries to provide birth control as a concomitant or even as a part of economic aid.

Often this opposition to the Church's views is based on a misconception due to ambiguous use of terms. The phrase "birth control" itself is used to mean population control, using any means from complete abstinence to sterilization and abortion, or it can be used to signify regulation of conception by means of periodic abstinence or artificial contraceptives of a mechanical hormonal or chemical nature.

There are six ways in which the size of a family may be restricted: (1) later marriages; (2) complete abstinence; (3) periodic continence; (4) contraception including the "contraceptive pill"; (5) abortion; (6) sterilization.

Normally Catholics understand "birth control" to refer only to 4. In this meaning it would be true to say that Catholics are opposed to birth control. Catholics also regard numbers 5 and 6 as immoral and therefore as forbidden means of influencing population rates of growth. It must be stressed that this is not, contrary to common opinion, a Church law formulated by clerics. It is a moral law which derives from the natural law, the law of the Creator himself which could not be changed by the Church even if she wished to do so.

But the Church is not opposed to population control, family limitation or regulation of births by means which she regards as morally acceptable if there are good, morally sound reasons why the birth rate should be reduced on the individual or national level. Catholics, like others, may differ as to the advisability of a particular attitude being adopted in certain cases. For example, an economist like Colin Clark might differ considerably from a demographer such as William Gibbons, S.J., as to the need or desirability of a restrictive birth policy.

The main difference between Catholics and others on this question is that the Church holds that family limitation may be practised in certain cases provided that the means used are morally acceptable; provided, in other words, that a couple do not resort to artificial contraceptives, sterilization or abortion. While this is the main difference, it is not always the only difference. Some outside the Catholic Church seem to have developed an anti-life bias and regard children—a number of children anyway—as an obstacle to the happiness of the partners, while others rate them as one of the elements of a good life, to be valued on the same level as a motor car or a better house. Obviously the Church with her views on the sacredness of human life and the privilege of cooperating with God in passing on the wonderful gift of life is opposed to these views. But there are many who share the Church's views on all points except with regard to the method of limiting the size of the family. They would regard contraception at least as on the same level as periodic abstinence, once the decision to limit the family for good reasons has been taken.

Why then does the Church oppose contraception, artificial birth control? Briefly, because it is against the law of God and also because of the moral and social consequences which it entails.

THE CHURCH'S TEACHING ON RESPONSIBLE PARENTHOOD AND PERIODIC CONTINENCE

The opposition of the Catholic Church to contraceptive birth control stems from the fundamental teaching of the Church that man is created by God and has an eternal destiny, that he achieves this eternal destiny by obeying an objective code of conduct laid down by God. This code of conduct can be found out by man's unaided reason in many cases, but Christian revelation—especially the teaching of our Lord himself—and the living authority of the Church have been given by God to help man to know what is right and wrong, God's will in his regard. In following the will of the Creator man is truly human, that is, he is acting in the way that God his Maker intended human beings to act.

Applying this to marriage and its use, Catholics believe that the very way God framed the human body with its two sexes, clearly physically complementary, shows what God intended. God intended the act of procreation to serve to reproduce the human race. The reproductive system is primarily designed for reproduction, to produce another human being with the sacred gift of life. The nature of the act of intercourse is to convey the male principle of life to the female organism so that it is possible for a child to be conceived. This is the nature of the act, intended by its Author. It must therefore be used in accordance with this design, if man wishes to act in accordance with the will of God and of his own nature. To interrupt the act, as in *coitus interruptus*, or to use a mechanical device or chemical preparation which prevents the act from fulfilling its natural purpose, namely the transfer of the male seed of life to the female reproductive tract, is contrary to the God-given design of the act. This is contraception and it is morally wrong because it is against the law of God. It is morally wrong in all times, in all circumstances, for all people.

The Church, basing her teaching on the law of God does not admit an empirical morality, one which changes with circumstances, where the good end may justify a bad means. The Church has on numerous occasions confirmed this teaching on the moral law which is written in man's own physical make-up. Pius XI in his Encyclical on Christian marriage condemned contraception and this condemnation was repeated by Pius XII as the following passage in his address to Catholic midwives in 1951 shows:

> In his Encyclical *Casti Connubii* of December 31st, 1930, Pius XI, of happy memory, solemnly restated the basic law of the conjugal act and conjugal relations. Every attempt on the part of the married couple during the conjugal act, or during the development of its natural consequences, to deprive it of its inherent power and to hinder the procreation of new life is immoral. No "indication" or need can change an act that is intrinsically immoral into an action that is moral and lawful. This prescription holds good today as it did yesterday. It will hold tomorrow and always, for it is not a precept of mere human right but the expression of a natural and divine law.

Pius XII also said, applying the teaching of the Church to our present subject: "Overpopulation is not a valid reason to spread the illicit practice of birth control."

This teaching of the Church, interpreting the natural law of God, may seem at first sight in particular circumstances to have very grave consequences on a personal, national or international level.   There are problems on all these levels to which only the use of contraceptive birth control seems capable of providing a solution, or, at least, an easy solution. Population pressure obviously gives rise to one of these crucial problems. But the Church believes that what is morally wrong cannot be scientifically right. Though she understands the humane motives which prompt a population expert such as the Indian Dr S. Chandrasekhar to say: "Whether it is moral or not, whether it is possible or not, birth control is necessary", she cannot agree. She firmly holds (and many experts confirm her stand) that there must be a way out of the apparent population dilemma—too many people, not enough food— without resort to means contrary to Christian morality. Her belief in Providence forbids her to think that God would allow a situation to arise, the only way out of which would be to break God's laws. In this she is not inhuman. On the contrary, she believes (and there is already evidence for this, as we shall see) that decisions which are based on moral principles derived from a study of the nature of man must conduce to man's true welfare.

There is not space for further treatment of this vexed question but readers are referred to several excellent books which go into the subject at length (see Select Bibliography at the end of this volume).

The negative aspect of Catholic teaching with regard to birth control is well known. Although it is founded on fundamental teaching, it *is* negative and gives only a partial idea of the beautiful teaching of the Catholic Church on Christian love and marriage and sex in the service of love. The idea of responsible parenthood flows from this teaching and refutes the caricature of the Church's doctrine which would make an ungoverned spate of unwanted births the consequence of her teaching on birth control. The Church stresses the procreation and *education* of children as the first end of marriage, responsible parenthood based on mutual love in its truest and noblest sense. The Church indeed exalts the mutual love of the spouses in marriage, comparing it to the love of Christ for his Church and even with the inner life of the Blessed Trinity. She regards the divine gift of sex as the means of expressing that love physically in accordance with the nature of man, body and soul. Such love excludes possessiveness, selfishness, fecklessness, lack of consideration. Such love could not lead to an irresponsible use of marriage, to a large family merely for the sake of numbers, or for the thoughtless satisfaction of instinctive urges. The family may be large but this must be due to a love of life, a desire to cooperate in the sacred task of handing on new life in partnership with God, a regarding of the good of each of the partners and the family as a whole. But in certain circumstances, this love may show itself in a smaller family, the result of a prayerful and realistic assessment of family needs and resources, the health and welfare of children and partners, even the needs of the community or nation.

Catholic teaching, if loyally adopted, cannot possibly lead to an excessive and haphazard population, for the Catholic husband is taught, provided the moral law on marital relations is preserved, to exercise self-control in marriage, not to overtax the strength of his wife, nor to procreate more children than he can hope to educate and rear healthily and to make suitable provision for every child he has, so that all his children may become healthy, vigorous and loyal citizens.

The means of periodic continence by which Catholics may achieve regulation of births is in accord with such love and the teaching of the Church. This method is much more than a technique but a deliberate rational means of regulating the size of the family which implies self-control in the service of love. The partners, with good reasons for doing so, make use of the times of the month when the wife is known to be incapable of conceiving. This method has become more and more accurate in recent years and is as "safe" as or safer than contraceptive methods. Many may see little difference between this and birth control in the accepted sense and may even accuse Catholics of hypocritically using a casuistic way out of their difficulties. Such an accusation could only come from mistaking ends and means, the nature of an act and the motives for it. Catholics teach that contraception is wrong, not because it is wrong, for good reasons, to control the size of the family, but because the means used are against the true nature of the act as designed by God. The good or morally desirable end, namely necessary limitation of the family, is achieved by a morally bad means, namely performing the marriage act against the designs of God. The Catholic might indeed sin by having morally wrong motives for wishing to limit his family, but, if he uses periodic abstinence, he safeguards the nature of the act, whilst even a good motive cannot make contraception morally right, because it is wrong in itself.

Abortion and sterilization have developed in recent years as a means of limiting population growth. These are equally morally unacceptable means because they interfere with the integrity of the human person and his acts. No one would deny that once conceived the embryo will develop and is intended to develop as a separate human person. The abrupt deliberate termination of this process is clearly contrary to the design of nature and morally wrong. It is depriving a developing human embryo, with a right to life, of that right. This is independent of the technical question as to when the embryo actually can be regarded as a human being with a soul. The right to life exists from the moment of conception and it is wrong for another human being to deprive it of that right. In Japan the evil physical, social and mental effects of a policy of abortion are now recognized.

Sterilization is the most effective means of birth prevention whether male or female sterilization is used. The temptation to use it in a population situation such as India's is great, precisely because the defects of contraception as a population remedy have been recognized. But sterilization is an unjustified attack upon the integrity of the person. The sacrifice of a member or function of the body is allowable when necessary on account of illness or accident.. But this is not the case in sterilization where there is no disease in the reproductive organs but when the operation is performed so that a man may indulge his sexual appetites and at the same time avoid the consequences. As Dr J. Marshall has said: "Man cannot exercise his responsibilities as a man by letting himself be unmanned. Or how can a woman regard herself as a woman when that essential thing which differentiates her from man, to which all other sex differences are secondary, is deliberately thrown away?" The social consequences of increases in promiscuity and social disease are no more desirable than the personal ill-effects.

It is sometimes difficult for those who do not accept the Church's teaching to be completely convinced by the moral arguments against contraceptive birth control. It may be well therefore to vindicate the Church's position on other grounds.

SOCIAL AND ECONOMIC REASONS
AGAINST CONTRACEPTION

Contraceptive birth control is not the easy, immediate, effective, acceptable way of coping with population problems that it is made out to be. The contrast is often drawn between the slow and the long-term agricultural and economic improvements compared with the immediate efforts of a drastic birth control policy. This is a false picture.

The experience of Japan in radically reducing its birth rate since 1948 and enjoying increasing prosperity used to be pointed to with approval. This is no longer the case as Japan has proved the failure of a policy of birth control in the most "needed" and most favourable circumstances. In fact, after ten years' trial, the results of their contraceptive policy have so alarmed the Japanese Ministry of Health officials that they are reversing the policy begun in 1948 with the Eugenics Law.

Seldom can any measure have been such a disastrous and costly failure. The intention was to make contraception legal and even encourage it so as to lessen the number of abortions, though these were also allowed by the law, in order to cope with the great population explosion which hit Japan after the war. The results speak for themselves. In a population of just under 100 million in 1958, according to a Japanese White Paper, there were 1½ million abortions. One population expert estimated a further one million unofficial abortions. If these figures are added to the number of live births, which amounted to just over a million, it is obvious that contraceptives, which had been freely available for ten years, and were even pressed on factory workers, so that the factory owners should not have to pay family allowances, had not proved successful in preventing conceptions or as preventives of abortions. In 1949, just after the law had been passed, there were only 246,104 abortions. The reason for the failure is not far to seek. A demographic survey by the Japanese journal *Mainchi* showed that abortion was six times more prevalent in families that used contraception than in others.

Puerto Rico was another country which seemed ideally suitable for the use of birth control, and with one of the highest birth rates in the world, it seemed obviously in need of it. A birth control campaign was introduced by the government in this heavily crowded and compact island in 1939. Yet with no woman living more than walking distance from a birth control clinic (the contrast with a huge country like India at once springs to mind) the birth rate remained high until 1956, when it dropped sensationally, by means of sterilization. In 1958, Dr Mayone Stycos found that 19·3 per cent of the women having babies in hospitals were being sterilized.

With regard to India, one may quote A. Nevett, S.J., who has studied the population problems of that country at first hand for many years. He says: "To this end, contrary to family planning propaganda, contraceptive practices will be of no avail since, on the avowal of family planners themselves, artificial birth control has received little acceptance among the masses. They admit that before it is widely practised a long period of propaganda is required." He might also have added that it will be used, as F. L. Brayne prophesied over ten years ago,[2] by the very ones in India who do not "need" it: the rich, the cultured, the intellectuals, who should now be producing the country's leaders. The very cultured Parsees, for example, are threatened with virtual extinction as a result of contraceptive practices.

A survey carried out in Lucknow and Jumpur showed this trend. The women who had at some time resorted to contraceptive practices were classified as follows:

		per cent
1.	Rich	32·7
2.	Middle	23·3
3.	Poor	9·1
4.	Very poor	0

This underlines the observation of Sauvy, Meier and others that a certain amount of social and economic development is necessary before artificial birth control can be practised with any appreciable success. Yet the very people who advocate birth control do so because, they say, agricultural, economic and social progress is not quick enough; the implication being that contraception is. In fact, several writers get themselves into the inconsistent position of seeming to want economic and social progress so that contraception could be practised, which would lead to social and economic progress! Catholics need not feel unduly inferior if they keep aloof from such campaigns.

The difficulties are realized by even the most ardent champions of birth control. Dr S. Chandrasekhar, the head of the New Delhi Population Institute, in his book *Hungry Peoples and Empty Lands* said:

> But taking the message of birth control to the rural millions is more easily said than done. As it is, the villages of Asia are starving

[2] He said, writing in 1948: "India is short of leaders and educated people; if artificial birth control were regularly taught, the first people to learn and practise it would be the very leaders and educated people of whom India so urgently needs more and more to help raise the general standard of living. Publicity and education are so backward in India that, before the knowledge of scientific birth control reached the general mass of the people, the shortage of leaders brought about by birth control would seriously handicap further progress in raising the standard of living."

for medical and health facilities . . . they are far removed from dispensaries or clinics. . . . A clinical examination, a contraceptive and the ability and willingness to resort to it may be centuries away from a hovel in India, a sampan in China, a rural hut in Japan.

Recent developments have not altered this judgement to any extent though intensive work has been done by the Family Planning Association there. There is considerable justification for the view that contraception, to be really successful, presupposes a certain level of education and economic development.

Misgivings among experts with regard to the short-term effectiveness of contraceptive birth control—and, as Paul Hoffman had warned, it is the short-term which may be decisive with regard to improving the lot of the developing countries—are now widespread.

Professor Glass,[3] himself fully in favour of the spread of birth control knowledge and techniques, sees a number of difficulties at the present stage and doubts if there is as yet much basis for expecting a rapid adoption of birth control and of small family patterns in many under-developed countries for the following reasons.

Quite apart from religious considerations, the decision to embark on a policy of birth control in a developing country is a delicate one to make. It does not appear in keeping with general ideas of progress, for fertility, virility and national pride still tend to be linked together. A deliberate reduction of 50 per cent in mortality rates would be obviously a good thing; it is not so clear that a 50 per cent reduction in fertility would be similarly acceptable. To some it may seem and indeed be a negative thing: that the pace of economic and social progress is not sufficient to take care of the alternative, expected population growth.

Opposition within the international agencies to the spread of birth control advice will also be an obstacle, while it would be

[3] See Symposium of British Association, *Hunger. Can It Be Averted?* pp. 15 ff.

very difficult to provide it on an inter-governmental basis.
President Eisenhower, for example, stated emphatically: "I
cannot imagine anything more emphatically not a proper
political or governmental activity or function of responsibility.
This Government will not, as long as I am here, have a
positive political doctrine in its program that has to do with
birth control. That's not our business."

And such strings to economic aid from one country to
another would be open to misunderstandings.

Finally, if birth control policies were adopted and assistance
of this nature requested and obtained, it would be unwise to
expect any sharp change in levels of fertility. As we have seen,
in spite of a very extensive birth control campaign in Japan, the
sharp reduction in the birth rate has been due largely to the
increases in abortion and sterilization (now estimated at
45,000 per year), to which this campaign led. Japan, moreover,
is not under-developed but highly industrialized. If one takes
a very low estimate of the combined totals of legal and illegal
abortions and reckons one and a half hours as the time
averagely needed for an abortion, then about three million
doctor hours per year are spent in the service of death rather
than life. This is bad enough in a country where there are a
good number of doctors. It would be disastrous and extremely
undesirable in under-developed countries, where, as we have
seen, there may be only one doctor for 50,000 people to look
after all their medical needs.

Aldous Huxley has pointed out in *Brave New World Revisited* that death control is comparatively easy while birth
control depends on the cooperation of an entire people.

> Birth control depends on the cooperation of an entire people.
> It must be practised by countless individuals from whom it
> demands more intelligence and will-power than most of the world's
> teeming millions of illiterates possess and (where chemical or
> mechanical methods of contraception are used) an expenditure
> of more money than most of them can afford. . . . For all these
> reasons death control is achieved very easily, birth control is
> achieved with great difficulty.

In addition, there is the danger of dissipation of money and personnel in giving this type of aid to under-developed countries. The amount of financial aid and technical assistance, as we shall see, to bring really effective aid to the under-developed countries to enable them to put into operation constructive measures to help them to climb out of their poverty, is limited. To add an extensive and costly scheme in money and manpower to promote contraception would be putting too much of a strain on the not too plentiful or too generous aid offered by the West.

It must never be forgotten that birth control is negative; it does not create anything, it does not make anything, it does not solve anything. It merely means that fewer people will be born into poverty-stricken circumstances which it is powerless directly to improve. No amount of birth control can stop the poor and hungry millions from existing. Their misery needs to be relieved by positive measures. Vitamin pills rather than contraceptive pills are what they need and they are more easily given, and, as we have seen, more directly and speedily relieve misery.

Incidentally, it would be premature to pass judgement on the so-called contraceptive pill (or rather pills, for there are a number of different types) which is really an anti-fertility pill. Although in clinical tests under Dr Pincus in Puerto Rico and other parts of the world, they have shown a very high success rate and no really harmful side effects have been observed (except a few deaths from thrombosis), reputable medical opinion is very cautious with regard to the use of them. Both the *Lancet* and the *British Medical Journal* have warned against the possible long-term undesirable side effects. The *Lancet*, indeed, said that twenty years may pass before we can assess the safety of the present oral contraceptive. Professor Sir Charles Dodds, President of the Royal College of Physicians, one of the foremost endocrinologists in the country, has given the gravest warning of the possible consequences of the use of the oral contraceptive. He said:

The continuous and cyclical use of these compounds may possibly have other undesirable effects which the trials conducted to date have not resolved. Such effects, for instance, when their use is continued throughout the reproductive period of a woman, might include the pituitary, mammary glands and ovary. . . . The fact that in a relatively short period nothing has been found does not really indicate very much. While everything might appear all right on the surface there may be deep-seated changes going on in the body. . . .

The experience with new drugs, which seemed to be adequately tested to the full satisfaction of the medical profession and which later proved extremely harmful, gives point to this warning. As I write in the middle of 1962, there is great alarm about the effect of a tranquillizer, Thalidomide, on pregnant women. A considerable number of babies born to women who have taken this drug have horrible deformities. And this drug, unlike the contraceptive pill, does not act directly on the reproductive system.[4]

There are also political and racial reasons which make the offer of contraception a very delicate matter. "Birth control, a plot to kill negroes", runs writing on a wall in Kingston, Jamaica. One does not need to take notice of writings on a wall, but these may indicate that the writing is on the wall in another sense: that the mother country, forbidding free entry of coloured immigrants, may seem to be coping with the resultant situation by restricting their numbers rather than by improving their conditions.

The Communists, apart from a short period around 1957 in China, appear as the champions of life and progressive growth and the West, offering contraceptives rather than food, would show itself in a weak light. Also for the white races, having reduced their own fertility, to offer contraceptives to the coloured races invites misunderstanding when the colour bar is by no means the dead letter that it should be. The fact that the Chinese, at their present rate of natural increase, will soon form one quarter of the world's population, illustrates the remark of

[4] The Family Planning Association in England, which had the "courage" to proceed with the contraceptive pill has now adopted a very cautious attitude.

Sir Charles Darwin in that to be really successful a population policy needs to be adopted universally otherwise imbalances appear. If India and Japan adopt and maintain drastic population policies, this may be seen later to have been imprudent in view of such projections.

Dr Glass sums up the practical conclusions, even for those who believe in birth control, that one can draw from what has gone before:

> Clearly far more work needs to be done, and equally clearly, until we have the results of this work, it would be unwise to base policies for economic and social development upon the assumption that fertility levels in the under-developed countries can and will be greatly modified in the very near future.
>
> A very realistic programme for international action in the field of development would need to allow for the continued increase of world population for a sizable period at around the rate of 1·7 per cent per year or higher.

The above considerations make it clear that the Catholic Church has many reasons, apart from her moral position, to distrust population policies based on artificial contraception. The accusation of special pleading sometimes brought against her apologists[5] is not so valid as the counter accusation of lack of a thorough thinking through of all the dangers and implications of their policy that might be brought against family planners.

---

[5] In an appendix to Chapter IV of my book *People, Space, and Food*, written in 1959, I quoted the opinion on "the pill" of a Catholic gynaecologist which was criticized: "No one has yet followed it up for sufficiently long to see whether it will still continue to have a contraceptive effect by suppressing ovulation, or whether resistance to the drug will be built up inside the body. Similarly, no one has yet followed it up for sufficiently long to see whether prolonged use of the drug leads to harmful effects. While, however, it is yet too early to give an authoritative medical opinion on the subject, it does seem that it surely cannot be a safe means of contraception and that it may well have harmful repercussions later on in a woman's life. The drug works by suppressing ovulation and thus interfering with the woman's menstrual cycle, and it is difficult to believe that one can change one of the most important endocrine functions in woman without causing some effect." This is similar to the judgement of Sir Charles Dodds, a non-Catholic, in June 1962, quoted above.

But the subject is too serious for controversy or the scoring of debating points. Recently Bishop James A. Pike, an Episcopalian bishop of California, has suggested that more research should be devoted to, and more funds made available for, making more certain and more safe the means of family limitation acceptable to all religions and cultures. There is every reason to believe that, if as much money had been spent on research into periodic abstinence methods of family planning, this method could have been made much more easy, "safe" and certain and might even, as Dr Stone, late Vice-President of the Planned Parenthood Association of the United States, prophesied, provided the time of ovulation on which this method depends could be accurately fixed, supplant conventional contraceptive methods.[6]

We are then faced, as we were at the beginning of this chapter, with the problem of world poverty complicated by the unprecedented population explosion.

[6] I have stressed elsewhere my very strong conviction that from a pastoral point of view, Catholics and others whose consciences are affected by population pressures and other reasons for limiting the size of their families should be provided with the latest information and instruction on moral means of doing so, possibly by medico-moral centres, specially set up for the purpose.

CHAPTER III

HUNGER AND POVERTY
CAN BE WIPED OUT

Are the resources of the world sufficient to provide the food and other necessities of life for all people of the world, with their increasing numbers, or are some bound to linger in semi-human conditions? If the answer to this question is the former alternative then only lack of labour and capital and the technical "know how," or the willingness to use these means, could condemn the poor and hungry millions of the world to continuance of their situation.

THE WORLD CAN FEED ITS PEOPLES

We can state at once, with the bulk of the real experts of the world on our side, that the earth has abundant resources to feed its present population and any foreseeable increase in it for a long time to come. Colin Clark, the director of the Agricultural Economics Institute of Oxford, has shown how the world could feed ten times its present population, and even very much more than that, at the present stage of our knowledge. Sir John Russell said in 1954: "There are sciences and techniques still in little more than embryo stage which may completely dispel our present fears."

It is important for this fact to be firmly established. In recent years there has been a revival of the pessimism about world food and other resources which was prevalent after World War II and which was spread by books such as William

Vogt's *Road to Survival*, and Fairfield Osborn's *Our Plundered Planet*.

In 1959 in his *Brave New World Revisited*, Aldous Huxley had the following passage, based on a paragraph of *Our Plundered Planet* written ten years earlier. Talking about world population he said:

> At the present rate it will double in less than half a century. And this fantastically rapid doubling of our numbers will be taking place on a planet whose most productive areas are already densely populated, whose soils are being eroded by the frantic efforts of bad farmers to raise more food and whose easily available capital is being squandered with the reckless abandon of a drunken sailor getting rid of his accumulated pay.

It cannot be stressed enough that expert opinion is far from showing this pessimism. At the Cardiff meeting of the British Association for the Advancement of Science in 1960 a group of distinguished scientists discussed the part that science could play in combating hunger and averting the catastrophic suffering inevitable if world population should outstrip man's power of producing food. The broad conclusion, technically speaking, was that hunger need not be feared for at the least the next forty years, and that it could be wiped out on present knowledge if this were only properly applied. Paul Hoffman has declared: "The most challenging, pervasive and explosive idea of this twentieth century is that poverty, and with it hunger, can be wiped off the face of the earth."

Many are pessimistic, as Dr Lamartine Yates, a high official of F.A.O., has said, as to the capacity of the under-developed countries to climb out of primary poverty and, capacity apart, as to their possibility to do so. They point to the apparently meagre mineral resources of many of these countries, the eroded lands and unfriendly climates, the rapidly expanding population on territory in many cases already overcrowded, the absence and impossibility of saving on a scale to provide the capital required, the hopelessness of finding enough exports to pay for needed imports of equipment for industry and many more equally convincing arguments.

It is no good seeking a head-on refutation of these arguments. It may, however, be pertinent to inquire what the outlook was in Europe 200 years ago when she started pulling herself up by her boot straps. Could it not be said that then her peoples were too poor to save on any massive scale, that her agriculture could not be made more fruitful and her people would not adapt to factory tasks and urban ways of life? And yet the revolution took place. Is the plight of under-developed countries today any worse than that of Europe in 1750?

True, there are no vast prairie lands in temperate zones waiting to be ploughed nor are there empty spaces into which to move surplus population on a massive scale. But Europe had gone far down the road to industrialization before she had recourse to importing food and exporting people.

Today agriculture has other tools for increasing production without having to rely on new acres by the million. Also the newer forms of power for industry—oi i and, still more, atomic energy—mean that industry can be located where people are, not vice versa. Moreover, there are nations standing by who have already modernized themselves and who can lend their skills and experience for the job.

All these things give solid ground for believing that, during the next 100 years, there could happen in the remaining two-thirds of the world what hitherto has happened in only one-third—a revolution in modes of living, in standards of living, social patterns, arts and skills, culture and thought.

If this be a fair assessment, it is just about the most exciting prospect for a century-to-be that mankind has ever faced. By comparison, most of our other preoccupations appear puny indeed: cold war, class war, colour prejudice and so on. What is almost within human grasp is nothing less than the abolition of primary poverty, the bringing of low income peoples, not to equality of income with the wealthiest peoples, but to within hailing distance, so there is no longer a wide social and material gap between them.

Nobody suggests, least of all Dr Yates, that to do all this will be easy or inexpensive. The problems of combating world poverty are immensely complex, and there is need for urgent action. Above all, there is need for awareness of the necessity of urgent action.

At first sight, after studying the facts outlined in the first two chapters, there seems much more reason for pessimism than optimism. The very vastness and diversity of the problems of under-development, instead of serving as a spur to action, may tend to lead to apathy and despair. It is therefore of great importance to establish the fact that this is a manageable problem, that it can be solved, that it will be solved, but only if men care enough. As Lord Boyd Orr has said: "The only practicable limitations to food production are the amount of capital and labour human society is willing to devote to it."

Perhaps the best way of studying the possibilities of increasing the standard of living in the under-developed countries and wiping out hunger and poverty is to concentrate first of all on the food and agriculture sector. Everyone agrees that the basic approach to an attack on world poverty and under-nourishment should come from balanced economic development. Scientific techniques, economic arrangements and adjustment of social institutions—all must play their part together. The long-term answer to the problem of hunger and poverty must be sought in a generally expanding economy with the right balance in each country between the various economic sectors. But as the problem of hunger is so acute and as most of the people, as many as 80 per cent in some cases, of the under-developed countries derive their livelihood from the land, agriculture is the key sector in any such development. In any case it must provide food for people and it needs to provide also the margin from which to start a process of capital formation. If, therefore, we see that food production can be vastly stepped up, that farming methods can be improved so that the tremendous gap between the yields of subsistence farming in under-developed countries and the over-production of the farming methods of developed countries can be made less wide, this would be a realistic basis from which to make an assessment of the possibility of the under-developed countries breaking out of the vicious circle of hunger breeding hunger and poverty leading to still more poverty.

Everyone is aware of the huge surpluses that are piling up in the more developed countries. In the United States alone grain worth nine thousand million dollars is being stored at a cost of one million dollars per day. These surpluses can, no doubt, and should provide emergency relief for extreme situations of famine in the poorer countries. They can also be used as an integral part of planned aid to help a country's economy by supplying opportunities for consumption, without the inflation that would arise from more wage earners being able to buy more locally grown food (which may be in short supply) and therefore forcing up prices. But these surpluses, even if they were all transferred—and the problems of doing this with regard to transport and international trade are extremely formidable—would only prove a stop-gap measure, though possibly a very valuable one. They would be harmful to the proper development of the under-developed countries if they were regarded in any other light because no country in this day and age should be expected to live on a food-kitchen economy or to take round the begging bowl for food to more prosperous nations.

But their very existence is a refutation of those who blame the niggardliness of the earth's resources in the face of expanding populations. They show that the good earth when properly managed and exploited with modern agricultural science can produce abundant food supplies.

The earth, then, can feed its peoples and we are not faced with the dilemma popularized by Vogt: birth control or starvation. This pessimistic attitude is in strange contrast to the optimism which is shown in most fields of science with regard to future progress. There is no reason why agricultural science should lag behind and indeed it is not doing so. Since the war, agricultural production has surpassed population growth. More land can be brought under cultivation and new methods of cultivation giving greater and better productivity of crops can be developed and extended. The very deserts can be made fertile (the current fashion for desert living in California illustrates this).

In spite of the pessimism of William Vogt recently repeated by M. Guerrin and others who warn that famine on a large scale awaits mankind, there are abundant resources which can be tapped to feed mankind and any foreseeable increase in its numbers. F.A.O. officials add their testimony to the ones already quoted from Colin Clark and the British Association. The pessimistic view is a small minority one; one suspects that in some quarters it is given undue publicity because it favours the doctrinaire views of extreme family planners.

The official view of the F.A.O., which has the services of leading experts throughout the world and a unique mass of information on this subject, is:

> In principle, the farmers of the world would be able to produce enough food to conquer hunger. They will have to modernize their equipment and methods, particularly in the under-developed regions; but this requires that modern science be put at the disposal of all nations and, not only as it is today, at the disposal of the few.

While there are no grounds for the pessimism that believes man is doomed to starvation in face of expanding population, there is no room for forced complacency and theorizing optimism. The fact that the world can feed many times its population does not mean that automatically even its present population will be fed adequately, or that this will be achieved easily, without considerable sacrifices and without considerable changes.

Indeed the task of the under-developed nations is precisely that outlined by the F.A.O.: to use agricultural science to increase production in spite of grave social, economic and political difficulties. The fact that it can be done is heartening. It does not mean that it will be done.

COMPARISON OF AGRICULTURAL YIELDS

A comparison of yields of agricultural produce will show the vast possibilities opened up for the hungry peoples, if better methods are used instead of the primitive techniques common in most under-developed countries. Japan, using fertilizer extensively, gets about 35 cwt. of rice per acre; India, using an extremely small amount of fertilizer, gets less than one-third of this. Japanese wheat yields are about 17 cwt. per acre; Indian about 5½ cwt. The average yield of wheat per acre in Pakistan today is no more than it was in England four centuries ago and only one-quarter of the modern yield. Experimental farms in India have shown that Indian soil can approach Japanese productivity with proper managements.

Tropical countries do not necessarily need European type cultivation, for example, crop rotation of a European pattern, to achieve rapid advance. But they need the benefits of scientific knowledge specially adapted to their needs.

AN AGRICULTURAL REVOLUTION NECESSARY AND POSSIBLE

The reason why there is such a shortage of food in the under-developed countries, especially of the East, compared with the abundant production of the West, is to be found in the difference between the productivity of modern rational farming methods and the amount that can be produced by primitive methods which sometimes do not include the use even of a scythe or spade or the rudest form of plough; with no knowledge of, or little use of, fertilizers, organic or synthetic, and with no attempt to use improved seed. An agricultural revolution is possible by concentrating on the improvements in land and husbandry which our present knowledge makes it possible to achieve. These improvements need not necessarily be sensational ones; there is no need, for example, to try and extend the farming techniques of the highly organized Canadian or American farmer to a primitive farmer of Africa or South America or India. In many cases, there is not the scope, nor certainly would there be the capital, to justify such a huge jump; but comparatively simple improvements can have tremendous effects.

For example, Dr Hambidge when he was a North American representative of F.A.O., said that if the same intensive agriculture were practised throughout east and south-east Asia as in Japan, there would be an immediate surplus production of food of such colossal proportions as has never been witnessed on this earth. It is not the niggardliness of nature that holds down production; it is the dead weight of outmoded economic and social institutions which do not fit the needs, but which are very difficult to change. If enough men wholeheartedly support the ventures which are designed to create new opportunities for mankind and to make better uses of the resources of the earth then civilization will not only survive the present dangers but will greatly add to its achievements.

The greater part of the agricultural land, for example, of India is so under-developed and relatively unproductive that there exists considerable scope for development if the right means are used. In Japan, where the density of population is greater than in India, much greater, methods of cultivation are rather those of the market gardener than of the farmer. By using modern fertilizer techniques and irrigation systems, yields are obtained which are six times greater than those of India.

There is no need to labour this point. An agricultural revolution which would banish hunger from the face of the earth is possible, and practically possible. How is it to be accomplished? There are two lines of attack. First it is necessary to put at the disposal of the under-developed countries resources of modern agricultural science adapted to the circumstances of the individual country. In some cases this may call for more study and research, but there is already considerable knowledge of what is needed and considerable numbers of measures immediately possible to achieve sensational increases of productivity. Then, secondly, to secure change in the pattern of social and economic life so that the best use is made of the possibilities of increasing production.

IMPROVEMENTS IN FARMING TECHNIQUES

The improvements that can be made in farming techniques fall under four main headings: they are directed firstly to increasing the productivity of land which is already under cultivation in most cases and which can hardly be added to, in a given country, without a great project, and without great efforts. There also remains the additional source of much greater food production in the marginal land and arid land and the unreclaimed land of the world, which to be reclaimed need substantially the same techniques.

The four headings are: (1) irrigation, (2) the use of fertilizers, (3) better seeds, and (4) mechanical aids.

Irrigation

Water is the key to the more productive use of land. Irrigation in places which are suitable for it brings untold benefits in the shape of two or even three crops a year of good quality where before only one was possible and sometimes not even that. Huge hydro-electric schemes, while having a big positive effect, have also a very big negative effect by controlling the waters of a river and preventing floods. There are also smaller schemes which can have very considerable results both in the quantity and quality of food produced and additional side effects, for example, fish can be bred in irrigation ditches or among the growing rice plants. This provides a most valuable source of protein in regions which lack this essential element of a balanced diet. There is also the possibility of smaller schemes helping individual farmers. In fact, with regard to water supply, as with regard to almost every aspect of increasing food production, the words of Mgr L. Ligutti, Vatican Observer at the Food and Agricultural Organization of the United Nations, are especially true: "A lot of little people doing a lot of little things in a lot of little places can solve many big problems."

The problem of hunger is the problem of millions of small villages throughout the world. In this connection, the work of Mr Harold Smith, a water engineer whose services were sought at the beginning of India's first Five Year Plan, is interesting.

In his thirty years' career, he has drilled over 6,000 deep wells in Latin America, the Middle East and the Caribbean. "Water", he says, "is the key to world prosperity. It means food in the world's larder—which quietens discontent and creates a climate for peace."

His work in India, as part of the first Five Year Plan of that country, is especially relevant. In the Punjab, where shallow wells provided an uncertain water supply for the arid land, Smith's study of the terrain revealed that the alluvial plain of this ancient province was not really arid. He was convinced that the hard-packed earth, the despair of agriculturists, covered a huge reservoir of millions of gallons of water slowly filtering through porous layers of sand and gravel on its way to the sea. Mr Smith, with his crew of four, set up his drilling machinery to prove the feasibility of tapping this huge reserve supply of water to make these plains fertile. He was so successful that in twenty-six months he produced 755 wells irrigating some 302,000 acres.

This phenomenal feat of well-drilling assured farmers in the area of two certain crops per year, and was the cause of a great increase of production of coarse grain, wheat and sugar. Thanks to his operations, 350,000 people are eating more food and buying more of the products from India's budding industries. In addition, Mr Smith trained Indian technicians in his methods and in the use of his machinery. When he left, there were seventy-two men so skilled that they could carry on his work, and more important still, train other Indians to do so. He was also commissioned to help the development in Iraq and completed 170 wells there in 1957.

Even smaller and much cheaper improvements can often bring considerable change to small areas. I hope I may be pardoned a personal digression here which is relevant to much more than irrigation schemes. With a few bags of cement and a local stone mason, I myself managed at a cost of £10 to bring a clean, constant water supply to several thousands of people who lived near my mission station in the heart of tropical Africa. Such small projects, multiplied by thousands or hundreds of thousands, could have a powerful impact on farming in thousands of villages.

It should never be forgotten that every part of the world is in some parish, with the people, at least his parishioners, normally having confidence in the parish priest and his helpers. Here is a tremendous potential of technical assistance. Missionaries and aid organizations should have much closer contacts. Missionaries should be more than ever convinced that feeding the hungry and the mal-nourished is part of their Christ-like mission, while government officials and aid organizations can provide them with the means of helping their flocks to help themselves in the battle against hunger and can make use of their special position to break down prejudice against new methods and even to change social habits.

In my mission, which was in grassland country, where there were hardly any trees—no firewood trees at all events— because of the primitive method of burning the grass to prepare the ground for farming, I grew a plantation of quick growing eucalyptus firewood trees. They cost me 1d. per seedling from the local agricultural officer and they were planted on un-cultivable hillside and reached maturity in three years. The local "mammies" soon got the point that my firewood was only 100 yards from my house, while they had to make a two to three hour journey with heavy loads for theirs, and that they could avoid this for an outlay of about 6d. to plant fire-wood trees around their own houses. This is just a small example of cooperation between the missionary and an agricultural officer for the benefit of the people.

But, of course, emphasizing what can be done by small and comparatively small schemes does not detract from the immense boons of larger schemes when such are possible and feasible. The Kariba Dam in Rhodesia, the Dez River Dam in Persia, the Aswan Dam in Egypt, all the big irrigation projects on the model of the Tennessee Valley Authority's huge dam which succeeded in controlling the flood waters of seven American states, restraining their perennial havoc, building up irrigation systems and producing a vast hydro-electrical potential and getting rid of a big "dust bowl", are wonderful means of increasing crop production, reclaiming land, manufacturing electricity and controlling flood waters. It is reckoned that only one-thirtieth of Egypt's land is cultivated—the land near the Nile. The High Dam at Aswan will extend the habitable land of Egypt by a few inches on the map, but it could bring, as the Gezira plan brought to the Sudan, food, prosperity and decent living conditions to hundreds of thousands of people.

Another example of what water on a big scale can do is provided by a project in southern Mexico, where the problem was one of dense jungle and constant flooding. The Papaloapan River Valley in southern Mexico extends over nearly 20,000 square miles in the states of Puebla, Oaxaca and Vera Cruz. Potentially, it is one of the richest agricultural areas of Mexico, but, up till recently, most of it was wild jungle subject to frequent flooding and its 1,000,000 inhabitants were impoverished. With fifty people per square mile the land was overpopulated.

In 1947, a 75,000,000 dollar multi-purpose development project was begun. At the town of Temazal a main dam was completed, which is more than half a mile long and 200 feet high. A dyke stretches for a mile and a half, and a vast artificial lake has been created. The danger of floods has been ended for the first time in man's memory.

In five years from the beginning of the project the production of wheat increased from 1,000 tons annually to more than 9,000 tons. The valley, which formerly produced 25 per cent of all Mexico's cane sugar and 80 per cent of its pineapples, has increased sugar cane production by 40 per cent and pineapple production by 85 per cent; a hydro-electric plant is supplying 650,000,000 kilowatt hours of power annually. More than 300 miles of roads have been built, malaria has been wiped out, and new towns, villages and schools are appearing in the jungle. Apparently the Papaloapan River Valley, with a growing population, is no longer overpopulated.

The Soviet Union has schemes such as the dam across the Amu Darya river near its delta at the Aral Sea. This will irrigate thousands of square miles of desert. Predicted yields from the irrigation schemes are, in millions of tons, wheat, eight; sugar beet, six; cotton, three; and rice, a half. In addition, there will be pasture for nine million sheep and two million head of cattle.

The Yellow River is at last to be tamed with incalculable benefits. This river flows for 3,000 miles through China and has been the scourge of that country throughout history with its recurrent severe floods. In 1938, one such flood cost the lives of nearly one million people and rendered over 12 million homeless. The plans are to harness the river and to control the floods by a system of forty-six dams. This would allow 20 million acres to be irrigated and produce 110 thousand million kilowatt hours of electricity per year. These multi-purpose dams, and others such as the Bhakra Dam in India and the Yanhee Dam in northern Siam, will lead to a vast increase in food potential and will also ease population pressures along the rivers and deltas. They are examples too of one way of reclaiming or extending cultivated areas.

A new development which is fast reaching the economic stage is the process of obtaining fresh water from salt water. There is little doubt that this development will go forward and may before the end of the century, possibly with the help of atomic energy, enable the oceans to be diverted to the irrigation of the deserts. Already there are some plants in operation in the world.[1] The use of this method by Israel is interesting as a supplement to the tremendous achievements of this new State in post-war years.

Israel has made an intensive study of its water supplies and has used all kinds of methods to develop them. Unsuspected reserves have been discovered and well borings made through-

[1] One English firm now markets a plant costing £300,000, which will produce a million gallons of sweet water per day at a cost of ten gallons for 1d.

out the country. But these have not been sufficient to develop the barren but potentially fertile plains of the Negev, and so water has been piped (by a massive scheme, assisted by foreign capital) from the Jordan and Yarkon rivers into the desert area of Negev, penetrating many miles into it and carrying irrigation and promise of fertility with it.

In addition, ways of turning salt water into fresh have been and are being investigated, to utilize the brackish water reserves underground and also (though this is a long-term project) even the waters of the seas which wash Israel's coasts. There are several processes for doing this. An ex-Russian engineer, Dr A. Zarchin, has developed a novel process for extracting fresh water from sea water which involves desalting by freezing. This, it is hoped, will be cheaper than the ordinary way of evaporation and distillation. Using steam power from power stations is another way. This is being tried out on the Red Sea, and it is hoped, by the use of the steam exhausts of electrical power plant, to distil over two million gallons of water per day at an oil-fired power station at Eilat. In the next ten years, Israel is planning to install 600–700 MW of new electrical generation power. If all these new power stations were coupled to sea-water distillation plants, the national water supply could be increased by 44,000,000,000 gallons per year.

A further possibility is an atomic reactor specially designed to extract fresh water by distillation from sea water. This holds great promise for the future and may be the means of completely solving Israel's water problem, and turning the whole of its barren land into fertile crop areas. Another scheme is to revive the ancient water conservation practices which are found all over the Negev. In biblical times, there were flourishing cities in what is now barren land, and the idea of reviving ancient Israelitic practices to settle the desert must obviously have a powerful poetic appeal for twentieth-century Israelis.

Other experiments, such as the development of plants which need little or no moisture, suggest other lines of progress for the desert lands of this enterprising new state.

There are difficulties in the use of water for irrigation and it is hazardous to try and increase water potential by means of wells dug haphazardly, especially without a study of the terrain, but more study and research are being given to the problem of water and arid lands which should obviate these dangers.

The use of fertilizers

The cultivated land of the earth can be extended very considerably to an extent which is difficult to estimate. The following is an assessment by Mr W. H. Pauley, an official of F.A.O.

In the temperate zones of the northern hemisphere and the intensively populated countries of eastern and southern Asia, there seems little possibility of expanding the area under cultivation. There are other zones where the agricultural potentialities have hardly been touched.

For instance, the continuously hot wet belt lying athwart the equator presents the most conspicuous gap in a world map of sedentary agriculture. Of this the English geographer Dudley Stamp has written (*Land for Tomorrow*, p. 60): "Over huge areas the equatorial lands are scarcely to be described as underdeveloped. They are literally undeveloped and largely uninhabited." This climatic zone covers the land masses of Africa and South America on both sides of the equator as well as the great outer islands of Indonesia and southern Philippines. It remains mostly jungle inhabited by a sparse population which subsists mainly on shifting cultivation. Though a few specially favoured areas, such as Java, have become intensely cultivated, the present distribution of population is due in the main to historical factors which no longer reflect the technological possibilities of the mid-twentieth century.

It is hardly necessary to say that there will be numerous difficulties in the effective utilization of these equatorial lands. The natural fertility of the soil is low, owing to the leaching by heavy rainfall, and it is particularly difficult to maintain organic matter and avoid erosion once the forests have been cleared. It is hardly conceivable, however, that, armed with the resources of modern science and wealth for research and investment, man will be unable to work out cropping patterns and methods of management which will enable him to build up and maintain soil fertility and so turn to good use the abundance of moisture and heat capable of bringing to maturity two or even three crops a year.

It is not yet possible to foresee what proportion of these equatorial soils can ultimately be developed for agriculture, nor how far ahead this development lies. When it does come we shall see in the equatorial lands of the Congo and Amazon basins, the untouched eastern slopes of the Andes and the great islands of south-east Asia, an agricultural revolution comparable to the opening up during the last century of the grass or lightly timbered lands of North America, Argentina and Australia.

The tropical savannah lands of Africa, South America and Australia, where high summer rainfall is followed by a long dry season, constitute another area of considerable agricultural potential. At present, these areas are used mainly for extensive cattle grazing and a tremendous amount of patient experimentation with soils, crops and pastures, conservation of water and fodder and large investments will be needed to render these lands productive. Nevertheless, a substantial portion of the vast areas involved are undoubtedly destined for much more intensive exploitation, including mixed crops and animal husbandry.

Substantial possibilities for expansion of cultivation are also to be found in the podzol zones of the U.S.S.R. and Canada. The potential importance of these zones cannot be compared with that of the unused tropics, but the development of mixed farming based upon adapted cereals, forage crops and a dairy industry, with the use of substantial amounts of lime and mineral fertilizers, can be expected to give a fairly large production of those crops and animal products to which the abundant resources of the tropics are less suited.

Even in the temperate zone, there exist extensive areas in the southern hemisphere (most notably in southern Brazil,

Uruguay and Australia) where extensive grazing continues to be the main use of well-watered lands potentially well suited to agriculture. In South America, land tenure and cultural traditions have militated against arable farming. In Australia, many of the areas, passed over by the pioneers as too infertile, can be rendered productive by the addition of trace elements and the growth of leguminous pastures to raise the nitrogenous and organic content of the soil, after which they could be brought under a system of mixed farming. It has been estimated that about 160 million acres of well-watered, reasonably level land in southern Australia await such improvement, compared with about 40 million acres which are now under crop or improved pastures.

The above illustrates the use of fertilizers as the next great source of a rapid increase in food production. This is one of the main reasons for the difference between the yields of the more advanced countries and the less advanced. One agricultural economist has even said that the whole of India's food supply position would be cured with extreme rapidity if sufficient fertilizer were available and applied to the land. It is true that the use of fertilizer is only profitable when we have a thorough knowledge of the nature and possibilities of different soils, but in many cases we have this and research is going on into the nature of tropical soils.

Chemical fertilizers are used hardly at all in most of the developing countries. For example, Asia, other than Japan, which has almost as great an area under cultivation as Europe and North America put together, uses only about half a million tons of fertilizer. In other words, the developed countries use thirty times more fertilizer than the poorer countries of the East. Not only does India not use chemical fertilizer, but she does not use the organic manure which would be more useful for her even than the chemical fertilizer, because dung is used for fuel. The growing of firewood trees would be a double boon in Indian villages, and would have a considerable influence on improving crops by releasing organic manure.

Better seeds

So important is the improvement that can be brought about by the use of better varieties of plants—better seed—that the F.A.O. inaugurated (in 1957) a World Seed Campaign and devoted a special year called World Seed Year in 1960 to it. It is relatively easy and cheap to get farmers to use improved strains of selected seeds, the fruit of research and technical "know-how", one of the most rapid and successful means of technical assistance. In fact, improvement of seeds, and more and better fertilizers, can transform the face of the valley or hillside in less than a year. The F.A.O. has numerous success stories to its credit in this sphere. For example, high-yielding Italian wheat was introduced into Yugoslavia in 1957. As a result, production increased by 30 per cent and Yugoslavia no longer needed to import wheat. The usefulness of a strain of wheat or any other crop specially suited to a particular area, with special qualities to resist plant diseases in this area, is too obvious to mention. Advances in hybridization, even using atomic energy, give grounds for believing that this may soon constitute a major "break-through".

Radiation can be used to produce changes in the structure of organic substances. In agriculture, radiation effects are being used to produce new plants, to preserve foods and to eradicate insect pests. New kinds of plants, such as flax with stiffer stems, which can be harvested mechanically instead of by hand, have already been produced. This has been done by using radiation to cause genetic changes; that is, some of the seed from plants subject to radiation grows into plants with different characteristics.

This very recent development in plant genetics promises the most astounding improvement in plant breeding that the world has ever seen. Radioactivity, it has been found, can be used deliberately to produce mutations in plant strains, and thus to develop scientifically useful strains which before were only the accidental results of long experiments, their production being beyond direct human control.

In the Biological Irradiation Group near Wantage, scientists are producing hundreds of artificially obtained mutations, by bombardment with gamma rays, in their search for bigger, better and healthier plants. These transformations are achieved by inch-long slugs of deadly "hot Cobalt 60" buried deep inside a four-foot wall. A new delicious super-cabbage has been produced in this way. A high-yielding red clover, useful for cattle food, has also been developed, and a cultivated tomato plant has been grown with the disease-resisting qualities of the wild variety. The United States, India, Italy, Argentina, Costa Rica and other countries have similar research projects.

This is all part of the work of plant geneticists to speed up the slow natural processes of evolution by using the new tools of the atomic age. It is as though, for evolutionary purposes, a thousand years had been telescoped into one. The world's first radioactive farm is already in operation at Brookhaven, Long Island, U.S.A. This laboratory farm has produced, for example, peaches, some of which ripen nine days earlier than usual, others three weeks later. An orchard planted with the normal types and these two mutations could have a staggered harvest, cutting losses from market gluts.

Of course, use of selected seed and fertilizer go together as illustrated in the following incident described by Noël Drogat in his book, *The Challenge of Hunger*:

In a country like India, where the basis of agriculture is the family farm, the women are closely associated with the work of the fields. They do not undertake the heavy work, but they do supply a large part of the labour for other tasks, such as sowing, planting out, weeding and even the building of terraces. People discuss the example of one village, where it was the women who persuaded their husbands to use fertilizers and selected seed. The advisor had failed in his task of persuasion and had turned the problem over to his woman assistant. It was the custom for the village women to plant vegetable seeds in pots in the hall where they met to do their sowing. The woman assistant planted a grain of wheat of the local variety in one pot and a grain of selected seed in another, repeating the operation in two other pots, each of which contained some fertilizer. To each pot she gave a name, so that they acquired

a sort of personality. The women watched the growth of the
plants as though it were a race and, when the corn was grown,
called in the senior farmers, good judges in these matters, to
declare which grain of seed had bred the winner. But there was
no need for a judgement; the superiority of the selected seed
grown in the fertilized pot was obvious. Now, the whole village
will use none but selected seed and swears by the use of fertilizer.

There is no need to think only in terms of increases in the
use of chemical fertilizers. The making of compost pits and
other ways of getting organic manure, the use of cover crops
and other improvements may be more suitable in areas where
manpower is more available than foreign exchange or the
products of rare fertilizer factories.

Mechanical aids

The use of mechanical equipment, mechanization, which ha
so vastly increased the productivity of the advanced farmer has
great potential for the under-developed countries, so long as it
is carefully worked out for each area. The introduction of the
scythe, for example, may result in three or four fold increase in
the amount that can be done by one man, in an area where the
only tool was formerly the sickle, as it did in a F.A.O. project in
Afghanistan. On the other hand, special tractors may clear
huge areas of ground in suitable circumstances. Ten million
acres of land were made suitable for cultivation by machines,
subsidized by the Colombo Plan, which destroy the deep-seated
weeds which render much of India's land in certain areas
uncultivable because the ordinary hoes cannot touch them.
There is not the need in the under-developed countries for
sophisticated machinery to increase sensationally output per
man; the need is rather to increase output per acre or to allow
acres of marginal lands to be used which otherwise could not
be cultivated. There is a great amount of manpower on the
land which cannot be siphoned off in a few years. Hence,
simple machinery such as a bullock-drawn plough, a hydraulic
ram easy to construct, or a simple water pump to replace
primitive and wasteful means of irrigation, will be more useful

in many parts of the under-developed countries. In this way too, farm machinery which we have grown out of could be used with profit. A second-hand obsolescent European or American drill might be much more useful than a new combine harvester. Simple improvements within the reach of most farmers can do much.

It must not be forgotten that in India in the reign of the Emperor Akbar, yields of wheat of a ton per acre were obtained compared with little more than a quarter of that today. Expensive mechanization may help in certain circumstances, but it is not necessarily a panacea for farming problems. This is not to minimize the rôle it could play. Why should we rely only on methods of farming of hundreds of years ago? But there is no need for huge, indiscriminate expenditures on tractors, etc. to raise crop yields, and past agricultural achievements are incentives to careful soil management using all methods, old and new, suited to the area.

Work against erosion may form part of irrigation schemes but it deserves special mention. The erosion of land and the bad management of the soil—the waste of the good soil of the good earth—were really the starting-point of William Vogt's pessimistic theories, for he is a soil expert. He reckoned that half of the good soil of the earth had been wasted by mankind and that the process was continuing. He did not allow sufficiently for the fact that this process can be reversed, and is being reversed, and that there are special international bodies concerned with nothing else than this reversing of the inroads of erosion and of desert on man's heritage of the soil. The earth is not like a coal-mine which is useless once it is worked out. Just as the earth can be spoiled by bad management, so can it be restored by good management.

All these scientific methods of improving farming are within the reach of the under-developed countries, with aid in money and manpower and knowledge from the West, and they are not so expensive as industrial aid will be seen to be. Yet they can transform the food situation, feed the hungry and give a margin for domestic saving.

It is easy and convenient to compare farming results in India and Japan as we have already done. These confirm the statement of Gove Hambidge that the introduction of Japanese methods could bring about a revolution in good yields, an agricultural revolution such as is needed.

Some idea of the net result of all these possibilities may be obtained if we contrast the situation in Japan, where the average farmer makes rather full use of existing scientific knowledge, with India where most peasants are only beginning to become acquainted with these possibilities. The production per hectare of arable land in Japan is approximately six times as great as in India. It is true that Japan has a very great advantage in that practically all the crop land can be irrigated, but it is also true that India and the other countries of southern and south-east Asia have a great advantage in their warm climate which is favourable to crop growth right round the year. In the very large areas of south-east Asia which could be brought under perennial irrigation, it may well be that a combination of scientific farming practices, assured water supply and a year-round growing season could result in an output per hectare which would exceed that in Japan.

ANIMAL FARMING

Arable farming has been stressed in this chapter. But there are great potentialities for improvement in livestock also. In India, of course, cattle are a great problem because they are regarded as sacred, but even so, apart from changing the social habit and religious customs of the people, much can be done. There are now stations in India where the strain and milk yield of the cattle are improved and dried milk is processed for distribution throughout India. The Oxford Committee for Famine Relief have helped to sponsor such a project in Annam.

In other parts of the under-developed world where the full potentialities of husbandry can be realized, there is great leeway to make up, pointing to sensational improvements in shape of more food if improvements can be made. The output per head of cattle in terms of meat, milk, and draught power is about five times as great in Europe as in the Far East or Africa, three or four times as high as in the Near East and two to three times as high as in Latin America.

FOOD FROM THE OCEAN

I have made no mention of food from the sea but this source of a rich and varied diet is at last beginning to be exploited in the developing countries, and could be an important source of protein and thus combat protein deficiency diseases. Recently, Israel doubled its catch of sea fish in two years. A new fish harbour has recently been built in Karachi and with the use of mechanized vessels should result in large yields, for the rich fisheries in the Indian Ocean have hardly been touched. Indeed, fish farming as a serious industry is still in its infancy. The Northern Hemisphere is 61 per cent water and provides 98 per per cent of the world's fish supplies. The Southern Hemisphere is 81 per cent water, and includes most of the poorer nations of the world, yet it provides only 2 per cent of the world's fish supplies.

Food from the ocean of a different sort, by harvesting the minute vegetable life of the ocean and processing it into a form palatable to human beings, is developing apace. Ritchie Calder in his *Commonsense about a Starving World* gives an interesting passage about this:

> The Japanese have long harvested sea growths and have used them extensively both directly and indirectly, to feed their population. Indirectly, for manure for their fields, and, directly as food for the table. At the Conference on "Science in the Advancement of New States," held at the Weizmann Institute in Israel in 1960, Professor Atuschi Watanbe of the Institute of Applied Microbiology, Tokyo University, described over 10,000 species of marine algae, seaweed and sea plants, which could be used as human food stuffs. He showed how they could be harvested and treated and, to demonstrate his point, served to the delegates Japanese delicacies. They were packaged in cellophane bags, like potato crisps, but they were wafers of crunchy seaweed preparations of various colours, brown, blue-green and red according to

the type of algae. They were palatable—if you like a slight flavour of iodine—and they were probably as nourishing as most of the processed breakfast cereals.

THE RAVAGES OF PESTS

So far we have considered the production of more food. But much of the food that is actually produced at present does not find its way into the mouths of the hungry. Human beings have to compete with pests for their food. Rats and insects and other pests ravage food crops that could feed millions of people. A few statistics show what a serious drain on food production they can be. Even in the United States, with good modern storage, it is reckoned that about 7 million metric tons of grain are lost in storage due to rats, while insects account for between 8 million to 16 million tons per year. Throughout the world, the F.A.O. estimates that the loss in food grains from these causes to be 33 million tons of essential foodstuffs. That is enough to feed the whole of the United States for a year. Or on a world scale, as Ritchie Calder says, "one out of fourteen persons in the world is liable to die of starvation for the lack of the food which these pests eat". Or again, one-tenth of the food crops in the United States is devoured before they are harvested. That means that field pests are consuming food equal to ten times what would be necessary to provide rations for the annual increase in world population of 54 millions. In 1959, the loss of food in this way in store throughout the world was 85,600,000 tons, which would have fed one-tenth of the whole population of the world for a year.

There are also a number of new discoveries which in their turn can add to the food supply of the world, such as nutriculture—the growing of crops in chemical solutions without soil. There are well over 100 nutricultural farms in the United States and throughout the under-developed world which are operating on a commercial basis. There are means of extracting protein directly from grass and other vegetable matter, instead of getting it from animals who have performed the process.

This has been a brief sketch only of the potentialities of increasing food production. The know-how exists to feed all the hungry. What is needed is an agricultural revolution to bring it about.

THE FREEDOM FROM HUNGER CAMPAIGN OF THE F.A.O.

This is the aim of the Food and Agricultural Organization of the United Nations and of numerous governmental and non-governmental organizations throughout the world. The Freedom from Hunger Campaign of the F.A.O., which is runing from 1960–5 with a World Food Congress in its central year 1963, is devoted to education and research and plans for action to make this revolution a speedy reality. Not that it is possible to have a "crash programme" in agriculture; this revolution must come quickly but it cannot be forced through. But this revolution is possible; it is urgent and it will come about if the peoples of the hungry countries and the well-fed countries get together, with the immense technical agricultural knowledge now available, to combat hunger in ways suited to the individual needs of the different areas of the under-developed world.

We need the "urgent patience" which respects nature's rhythm. Agriculture cannot be organized like a production factory. Nature is impatient of "blue-prints". It is not too fanciful to suggest that the failure of Russia and China in agriculture may be due to the fact that Marxism does not understand agriculture. It is an urban theory worked out by a man who knew nothing of the countryside and the natural links between a peasantry and the land.

Nevertheless, there is no reason why with concerted effort and respect for nature huge strides forward should not be taken. This campaign is an illustration of the awakening interest in agriculture as well as an effort to feed the hungry. With twenty years' experience and some of the best technical experts in the world, the F.A.O. may be indeed poised for a "break through", if, as seems likely, the Freedom from Hunger Campaign gets the support it deserves.

The Freedom from Hunger Campaign is intended to focus attention on the needs of the less-favoured countries, to show how these needs can indeed be relieved and to arouse public opinion in the more favoured countries so that these huge problems will be attacked with the massive assistance they deserve and which could ensure success.

The campaign will be waged on three fronts: the information and education front, the research front, and the action front. Education and information will be aimed at bringing about in the more advanced countries an informed understanding of and an intelligent sympathy with the problems and needs of less advanced countries; within these countries themselves it will aim to create a broad general appreciation of the avenues of progress awaiting bold and confident action. The research front will intensify the search for solutions to problems of agricultural development in individual countries and regions. The action front will seek to develop concrete projects to be carried through in individual countries, which would range through the whole field of food distribution and consumption, and would include measures to enhance the buying power of those countries most in need of more and better food.

This five-year campaign was substituted for the idea of a Freedom from Hunger Year in 1963 which Dr Sen originally proposed. It is obviously more satisfactory to tackle the immense problem in this way. 1963, with its culminating point of a World Food Congress, will be the central year of the campaign, but the fact that it will not be only a "Year", similar to the World Refugee Year, will enable interest to be sustained longer and will highlight the fact that the attack on world poverty and hunger does not consist in bringing charitable relief of a temporary nature. It is clear from what has been said that what is needed in areas where food is chronically scarce is to break the vicious circle of poverty and stagnation and enable the local people to fend for themselves. Such action must be initiated locally but, if it is to be successful, it will need very great outside assistance for some time to come.

The work of F.A.O. in this campaign will not be to supplant the work of the various existing organizations of a governmental nature and non-government organizations working for the same ends but to coordinate and supplement their work.

SOCIAL AND POLITICAL CHANGES

As I suggested at the beginning of the chapter, this involves not only utilizing the techniques which are available, but the training and educating of farmers slow to change their social customs which need to be respected but transformed.

Many conditions, social and political as well as economic, are required to be fulfilled in working towards this inspiring goal of an era of plenty for the world. For the results of agriculturally applied science and technology to be effectively distributed throughout want-ridden sectors of a lesser-developed region, and for these results to be absorbed lastingly and cumulatively by the whole human and social framework of a region, certain economic and institutional conditions have to be established.

Among the most crucial of these conditions are good systems of land tenure, provision of adequate and stable prices to agricultural producers, farm credit facilities, adequate marketing facilities, including cooperatives, and a general expanding economy, with the right balance in each country, between the various economic sectors.

Much research and experiment is going into the problems of how this should be done. Community development projects, credit unions and cooperatives,[2] work of extension farming officers, are some of the ways in which modern agricultural science and equipment can be brought to the village farmer— and this is a problem of many, many, villages rather than a

[2] See the chapter by Mgr F. Smyth in *Christian Responsibility and World Poverty*, edited by the present writer, Burns and Oates, London, 1963.

huge global problem. In developed countries, for example, there are extension officers for about every 700 farmers; in West Africa, the proportion is about one for every 4,000 farmers. The provision of extension officers depends, of course, on education—especially secondary education. Good progress is being made on these lines in parts of Asia and a programme for the multiplication of agricultural schools for training extension officers has just begun in Asia.

The problem of communicating new knowledge to illiterate farmers naturally has great difficulties. Sometimes, these difficulties may be exaggerated. The experience of Japan shows that even very small-scale, illiterate farmers can double their yields given instruction and other help. It took the Japanese nearly fifty years to do this. There is no reason why it should take so long with an all-out effort in the under-developed countries with sufficient help from outside.

I have spent considerable time on the need and possibility of an agricultural revolution because of its great necessity and urgency and also because until recently, and even now in some quarters, agriculture has been the cinderella of government departments. It is interesting that in the third Five Year Plan India is again laying great stress on the need for increasing agricultural output and is devoting more resources to developing it. Often in the emerging countries, this department has not had the prestige of other departments and has been given to someone not of outstanding ability or importance.

Mgr Ligutti has given three fundamental causes for hunger: (1) Lack of the knowledge of the potential of God's gifts to man; (2) lack of the will to apply knowledge and effort; (3) lack of social distributive justice. All these fundamental causes can be remedied by education, by a change of mind and a change of heart. A revolution of ideas must precede and accompany the agricultural revolution.

CHAPTER IV

THE ECONOMIC

REVOLUTION

The agricultural revolution which is necessary in most of the
under-developed countries of the world cannot take place in a
vacuum. It would not be desirable even if it were possible. The
balanced development of a nation's economy is essential for
its survival in the twentieth century or, at least, its survival in
conditions which will allow it to give a reasonable standard of
living in keeping with their human dignity to the inhabitants
of the country.

THE GREAT PROBLEM OF THE
TWENTIETH CENTURY

As I see it, the great problem of the second half of the
twentieth century with regard to the under-developed
countries is to enable them to achieve self-sustaining economic
growth without the gross social injustices of countries such as
Victorian England and other nineteenth-century and early
twentieth-century industrial countries witnessed, and at the
same time to avoid the harsh, brutal, demoralizing forced
savings of the Communist régimes.

TEMPTATIONS TO MARXISM

It is surely one of the supreme ironies of history that Marx's
horror at the treatment of the proletariat in the process of

industrialization of the nineteenth-century European countries should have led him to formulate a theory of economic history and view of the future which, in the hands of Lenin and Stalin, debased the farm workers and proletariat much more than the old economists' concept of the "economic man". It is strange, even now, to find that the revulsion from the nineteenth-century capitalism and its horrors often causes those with liberal ideas to tend towards the economic authoritarianism of the extreme left or Communist régime. Behind this is the knowledge that the process of preparing for "take-off" into self-sustained economic growth is a drastic one; it needs immense efforts and, to be quite honest, it seems to many to be more easily achieved when there is a strong central government which does not pay over-much attention to the rights of the individual. However much one may respect the tradition of Western liberalism, and freedom, it is very tempting to think that if one could, at one fell swoop and by no matter how stringent means, get rid of the effete landlord class, the rapacious money-lender (though his rôle is not always an unequivocally bad one) and the mass of social and religious prejudices and superstitions which hamper progress such as, for example, the exaggerated reverence for the cow, the monkey and the rat with their agricultural depredations in India, then state dictatorship, though one may pay lip service to opposition to it would have been a good thing. Andrew Shonfield has expressed this well in his *Attack on World Poverty*, where he says that there is a temptation to feel that it might not be a bad thing to let the developing countries go through the Communists' mangle, if only to achieve the progress that comes from the high rate of savings which are necessary and which such a régime could enforce ruthlessly. He concludes that countries suffer so much in the process that one could not allow such a defeatist attitude.

Also the experience of China in the last few years, in spite of the fact that there have been a good few natural misfortunes and quite a considerable amount of really bad luck, does not suggest that the progress achieved under a dictatorship is necessarily higher and more sustained than that achieved under a free government such as in India.

Stalin's agricultural policy is something which Soviet Russia, for all its tremendous leap into the industrial scientific and technological age, and the Russian economy, has not yet lived down and which is the source of recurrent crises not only in the economy of the country but in the political "set-up".

COMPARISON OF GROSS NATIONAL PRODUCTS OF POOR AND RICH COUNTRIES

In considering the economies of under-developed countries, the very first and most important thing to realize—something which has not always been realized by even the best writers on this subject in the past—is that we must avoid any generalization. One speaks of numerous countries with well over a thousand million inhabitants which need development. Global figures are used constantly as if they represented people with homogeneous problems. It is good to bring home the magnitude of the task by considering the numbers of countries as a whole which need to develop if they are to form a responsible part of the world economy, but the problems want breaking down into the problems of individual countries, often enough into the problems of individual areas of individual countries.

The poverty from an economic point of view of the less developed countries has been indicated on the basis of average *per capita* income—a rough yardstick it is true, but one adequate enough to give an idea of how appallingly and distressingly low the standard of living must be for many in these countries. It may be helpful to give a few details with regard to the national product of these countries—what they produce—and compare this with that of the more advanced countries .

N. Ginsburg calculates, in his *Atlas of Economic Development* (1961), on the basis of data relating to ninety-six countries in 1955, that the world average Gross National Product (G.N.P.) *per capita* expressed in dollars amounts to

200 dollars. The highest figure is that for the United States with 2,343 dollars *per capita* and the lowest for Nepal with 40 dollars, India having 72 and China and Pakistan 56 dollars. Out of a world population of 2·6 billion in 1955:

23 per cent or 600 million had G.N.P. of over 569 dollars
18 per cent or 500 million had G.N.P. of between 200 and 569 dollars
69 per cent or 1,500 million had G.N.P. of under 200 dollars

From the statistics put out by the O.E.C.D. and quoted in the two tables given below, it emerges that it is possible to compare the wealth in 1959-60 of the industrialized countries with that of the under-developed countries:

Table 1—*Distribution of gross national product and population in world economy, 1959–60, in % of world totals:*

	Population	G.N.P.
European countries of O.E.C.D.	11	22
North America	7	26
Japan, Australia, New Zealand, South Africa	4	7
Sino-Soviet Bloc	34	25
Other countries	44	20
Whole world.	100	100

This unequal distribution of available goods is further accentuated by the high rate of demographic expansion of many under-developed countries as well as by an economic growth that is slower and starts at a much lower level. These factors in

Table 2—*Estimates of the average rates of annual growth of population gross national product, and per capita gross national product 1953-9*

Regions	Population (growth rate)	G.N.P.	Per capita G.N.P.
Western Europe	0·9	4·5	3·6
North America	1·8	2·5	0·7
Japan, Australia, New Zealand, South Africa	1·5	7·1	5·6
Latin America	2·4	5·1	2·6
Africa	2·3	4·1	1·8
Middle East	2·2	4·8	2·5
Far East	1·6	3·7	2·5
Sino-Soviet Bloc	2·2	7·1	4·8
The world	1·8	4·7	2·8

combination account for the widening gap between rich and poor countries that is shown in Table 2; for the period 1953–9 the rate of annual *per capita* growth in the gross national product was 2·8 per cent for the world, 3·6 per cent for Western Europe and only 1·8 per cent in Africa and 2·1 per cent in Asia.

Figures such as these must doubtless be used with circumspection, on account of the gaps they contain and the difficulties that exist in estimating and comparing statistics of gross national product for a number of different countries; but they do bring two facts to light. In spite of demographic pressure and the difficulties of the take-off, the standard of living in under-developed countries is gradually improving. However, they are not catching up with the rich countries. The gap is widening. Another way of showing impressionistically the position of the under-developed countries is Paul Hoffman's, in which he says that the statistical income per person in the 100 countries and territories in the year 1950 averaged approximately 90 dollars, and that it had probably reached slightly over 100 dollars per person in 1959. Gross income grew at the rate of 3 per cent per year but because there were 200,000 million more mouths to feed in these countries in 1959 than there were in 1950, the net increase in income per person was only about 1 per cent, that is about 1 dollar a year. This is too slow—dangerously slow.[1]

AID FOR DEVELOPMENT NECESSARY

These figures also prove, more convincingly, I think, than any lengthy argument, that the economic development of the under-developed countries needs greatly to be speeded up if widespread misery and despair are not to accompany increasing population; that no matter how grave the need may be, and how inadequate the resources of the under-developed countries may be as shown by their appallingly low income, economic development must be primarily the concern of the developing

[1] Cf. J. Mertens de Wilmars "The Economics of Aid to Less Developed Countries", in *Christian Responsibility and World Poverty*.

countries themselves; that in spite of this fact, great, indeed, massive, generous, controlled, technically assisted, financial aid will be necessary for some considerable time before these countries are able to take off into self-sustaining economic growth which must be the goal of all activities both within the developing countries and from the developed countries assisting them. In a later chapter, I will discuss this aid to the developing countries as an imperative of Catholic principles of social international justice—a work of justice, charity and prudence—as Pius XII called it. In the meantime, from an economic point of view one may remark that it is in the interests of the developed countries to provide this aid. Using Paul Hoffman's figures, 1,250 million consumers are better for the economy of the world in the long run, than 1,250 million paupers.

Indeed, Paul Hoffman has pointed out that if the less-developed countries received additional foreign capital and increased local savings to a sufficient degree to lift their *per capita* incomes by only 1 per cent more per year over the coming decade, they might well offer to the United States alone a market for an estimated 14 billion dollars of its exports in 1970. This would represent an increase of more than 100 per cent over total United States exports to the same areas in 1958. But over a ten-year period, the total exports of all the developed countries to those areas, given this increased rate of economic activity, might be as much as 3,200 billion dollars. In the long view these 100 under-developed countries are, for the United States and for the developed nations generally, a great, a new economic frontier. It would be true to say that it is only since World War II that the awareness of duty and enlightened self-interest of contributing to the development of the developing countries has taken hold.

In the 1950's, the richer nations devoted substantial sums to this purpose. Indeed private investment and public grants and loans, including those from the World Bank, totalled around 30 billion dollars—a formidable sum. The results were, they must have been, if we consider the 1959 figures, meagre in the

amount of actual development which took place. There is no
doubt that increasing population contributed very much to
make this so. But it is also true that aid given was not directed
always or mainly to the economic development of the countries
that received it. Andrew Shonfield has shown how this great
figure comes to be whittled down when one analyses how much,
or rather how little, of it reached the countries that really
needed it but which had little to show in the way of military
necessities or economic profit as a justification for being recipients of it.

AN ORDER OF PRIORITIES

There is no doubt too that this new phenomenon of giving
aid to the under-developed countries was accompanied by
much naive thinking. The 1951 Report by famous economists
almost gave the impression that money alone was sufficient to
solve problems, and that the amount of money needed to
industrialize each person could be calculated and thus the
total capital sum needed for aid could be worked out.
Machinery of whatever kind and no matter how suitable, or
unsuitable, was often regarded as a means to help a country
to develop whether its economy was prepared to put such
machinery to use or not. There were a number of disillusion-
ments in the fifties and they have given rise to the criticism
made by opponents of aid who ridicule the equipment rusting
on the docks of some Eastern countries, or the tractors and
other machinery out of use because there was no one to maintain them. And one can point, as Andrew Shonfield has done,
to great prestige works completely unrelated to the capacities
of the country, such as huge airfields without the personnel to
run them and great hospitals such as that of Lima in Peru,
which are virtually abandoned because there are not the doctors
and nurses to staff them. Not only that, but the United States,
which was the most generous in granting aid—and within the
next decade one may surely hope that the countries who re-
covered from the devastation of the war by the generous help

of the United States will join her much more wholeheartedly in the sixties—found that aid did not always have the political or even social effects that were expected. Americans were disillusioned by the rancour and jealousy and criticism which their immense generosity often seemed to arouse, generosity which proceeded in many cases from the highest ideals, but which unfortunately, at times was not disassociated from the more hard-headed business methods of what looked to the sensitive under-developed countries as economic imperialism. Again, often enough, the very aid given had to be administered by political régimes leaving much to be desired with regard to integrity and even with regard to political morality. Sometimes, it seemed as if American dollars were bolstering up régimes which should not have been bolstered up and the inflation consequent on the influx of dollars made the lot of the poor people, whom the aid should have reached, worse still.

One can react to a situation like this in two ways: as Professor Bauer has done, for example, with regard to India; in his book he suggests limiting aid to a minimum; or one can, and I feel this is the saner approach, regard the defects of the fifties as the growing pains of the new approach to the under-developed countries, perhaps inevitable when the Western countries were first taking up the great challenge of the second half of this century. In that way, the mistakes of the fifties could provide and indeed I believe, have provided valuable lessons for the efforts of the sixties. As a result I believe that we are already poised for a much greater and more realistic effort to help the under-developed countries.

What should be the principles then that govern our attitude to the developing countries and to the aid which we should give them? No matter what form the aid may take, or how much it may or, indeed, should be dictated by a charitable attitude, it must not be an expression of paternalism, still less an offshoot of economic imperialism. Charity may prove the motive force for aid to the under-developed countries, but charity alone in action might be spasmodic and lacking in the necessary continuity. And economic assistance in the guise of charity tends to sap self-reliance. Food-kitchen economy has no place in the twentieth century except for emergency relief. It is out of keeping with the human dignity of developing nations and is not adequate to the huge problems involved. In fact, it is true to say that foreign aid can only help those who are determined to help themselves, though it may indeed often even be the task of the more privileged nations to educate these countries to an awareness of their needs and to a determination to help themselves.

The hard facts of economic life cannot be changed by charity alone or by moral indignation. This is as true on the national level and on the international level as it is in ordinary life. If a person is not responsible enough or, for some reason, is not able to use money given to help him and his family, it is waste of money to give it to him, and some other means of help must be found.

This thought is no doubt behind the concept of an order of priorities described by Andrew Shonfield in his book, *Attack on World Poverty*. No one would accuse this humanist economist of lack of concern for the misery of those in economic stagnation, but he very realistically says that the limited aid which is likely to be at the disposal of the developing countries should be available to those who will make the maximum use of it and who are at a stage of their economic development which will enable them to do so. The attitude governing the relations between the developed and under-developed countries must be one of partnership not of economic or political dependence. Thus, economic assistance should be divorced from international politics; it must not be used to buy goodwill or to gain an advantage in the Cold War and there should be no competing programmes either within countries themselves or even within the international agencies.

UNITED NATIONS AGENCIES AS CHANNELS OF AID

It is a good thing, as President Kennedy has said, to help the developing countries, and we intend to do it because it is the

right thing to do. And President Eisenhower had already said:
"If we grasp this opportunity to build an age of productive
partnership between the less fortunate nations and those that
have already achieved a high state of economic advancement,
we will make brighter the outlook for a world order based
upon security, freedom and peace. Otherwise the outlook will
be dark indeed. We face what could be a turning point in
history and we must act decisively."

Aid to the economies of the under-developed countries must
be based on knowledge. Lavish aid, even if it were available,
expended on countries whose resources in materials and
people could not absorb it, is of no avail and is the cause of
much waste and disillusionment. For this reason, greater use
should be made of the agencies of the United Nations which are
in a position objectively to study the resources of a country and
in cooperation with the government of the country to make
realistic plans. As Paul Hoffman said: "Representatives of
countries receiving assistance repeatedly declare their general
preference for help through the United Nations, for one reason
or other. For from this source, it is much more acceptable
politically; further, the United Nations assistance is a completely cooperative endeavour with a voice given to countries
whatever their size or wealth and with all countries contributing
to the costs. On the other hand, the United Nations can be
tough with the under-developed countries without being
accused of seeking any political or commercial advantage.
Better results can be obtained through the United Nations
machinery and substantial savings in money, and in the
United Nations and its thirteen specialized agencies reposes
the richest experience that can be found anywhere in virtually
every field of developmental activity."

But it must be recognized that the United Nations agencies
themselves were framed for much more limited objectives than
the huge programmes and administration of the massive capital
which is necessary to enable the under-developed countries to
become economically viable. And, therefore, a reform of the
organization of some of these agencies and the way they

function would be a necessary prerequisite to getting the utmost efficiency from this channelling of aid through the United Nations. Moreover, everyone agrees that very much aid will come through private investment and inter-governmental agreements and there must be no doctrinaire empire building on the part of international agencies. These problems are so huge that there is room for every possible kind and variety of assistance, even including means (provided they are acceptable to both parties) which are frowned on by some economists and political thinkers, such as the often despised tied loans, economic preferences and so on. There must be no narrow idea of how and when aid should be given. The target is a balanced development of these countries where agriculture, economic progress and social progress should advance hand in hand. We must never let ourselves in our thinking be concerned solely with economic advancement only, otherwise we risk, for the best possible motives, emulating the nineteenth-century Victorian economist or the twentieth-century Stalinist or Chinese Communist.

These countries must help themselves to a great extent; they have to work out their own salvation. Economic realities mean that these countries must earn by their exports a larger part of the foreign exchange required to finance their imports from the developed countries. There are a number of countries which already have made considerable progress: India and some of the Latin-American countries. For them the costly stage of investment has been reached which must be measured in millions of dollars rather than in hundreds of thousands, but there are other countries which are not yet in a position to absorb large amounts of capital. Most African countries would fall into this category, and there are other countries which, because of their material resources, will probably attract ordinary business investments.

THE NEED FOR GOVERNMENT ACTION

One does not need to be a doctrinaire socialist to realize that many activities absolutely essential to the development of the under-developed countries will have to be promoted under government aegis: almost all the investment that comes under the heading of infra-structure comes into this category and also a large part of what would be undertaken in more developed countries by the entrepreneur will have to be done through governments because of the lack of a sufficiently large and experienced merchant and management class in the under-developed countries.

The need for technical assistance is as vital as for capital investment but these must not be regarded as alternatives, that one either helps with money or with technical assistance. The stress in the fifties was on money, as if money could do everything; there might be a temptation in the sixties to stress technical assistance in opposition to money. This is especially a temptation when the balance of payments worries so many developed countries. It might be much easier to set up a department of technical assistance, as was done in Britain, rather than provide money even for a well-developed plan. In the same year that this new department under Mr Frank Vosper was set up in England, Julius Nyerere of Tanganyika was refused £24 million for a realistic programme of development for one of the most settled emerging countries in Africa.

HOW MUCH AID?

The need for economic aid has been clearly established and the spirit in which it should be given indicated. Two practical questions remain. How much aid do the developing countries require, and how much are they able to absorb? Is this possible for the West to achieve?

Various estimates have been given and these vary somewhat, as is only natural. The figure given by Paul Hoffman, the managing director of the United Nations Special Fund, which aims to double the national income of the under-developed countries in the sixties, is 3 billion dollars per year of extra aid. Most estimates would approximate to this. Professor Tinbergen gave a figure of 4 billion dollars but he had a few more countries in his estimate.

Barbara Ward has suggested the scale of aid needed for India, perhaps the most promising, and the most crucial field for Western economic assistance. She reckons that £400 million sterling per year is the minimum level of foreign assistance without which the very modest targets of growth cannot be achieved. A "big push" designed to make success certain and bring about economic independence more speedily might double the figure.

If we fix the minimum level of aid to India at about £2,000 million for the five years, the optimum figure at £4,000 million, even the larger figure represents no more than about two-fifths of 1 per cent of the West's combined national incomes during the period. It is perhaps not one-sixtieth of what they spend on arms. If the wealthier nations, say, those with *per capita* annual incomes of about £185, took up the old UNRRA yardstick again and agreed to give 1 per cent of their national incomes each year to economic assistance—surely not a crippling proportion—then the annual sum available would reach about £2,100 million and it would have been contributed, with even justice, from all wealthy sources, not—as today— overwhelmingly from the United States. An international

Table 3—Western national income: 1958

	National income (£ millions)	Per capita national income (£)	One per cent of national income (£ millions)
Australia	3,927·1	498	39·2
Austria	1,401·4	198	14·0
Belgium	2,895·0	212	28·9
Canada	9,028·5	517	90·2
Denmark	1,461·0	323	14·6
France	13,055·7	292	130·5
West Germany	14,437·8	276	144·3
Holland	2,296·4	255	22·9
New Zealand	952·5	417	9·5
Norway	1,087·5	318	10·8
Sweden	3,462·1	467	34·6
Switzerland	2,376·0	458	23·7
United Kingdom	23,095·7	447	230·9
United States of America	130,714·2	747	1,307·1
Total	210,190·9		

convention, specifying a 1 per cent contribution, would draw
in hopeless laggards like Western Germany, and relieve some
of the pressure on the American balance of payments. Table 3
gives a rough estimate of what the various national contributions might be.

India's share in such a programme would be dictated by its
sheer size. Since 40 per cent of the population of the under-
developed, non-Communist lands live in India, an Indian
proportion of two-fifths would not seem unreasonable. This
would yield at least £800 million a year in foreign exchange—
enough to fulfil the more ambitious of the alternative scales
of aid and yet still leave ample funds for other areas. And even
so, India, with twice the population of Western Europe, would
still receive over the five years less support than did the
Europeans during the four years of the Marshall Plan.[2]

The needs and possibilities of other countries making up the
remainder of the total of 3 billion dollars extra annual income
have been carefully analysed by Andrew Shonfield to whose
invaluable book, already mentioned, the reader is referred.
The 3 billion dollars needed might be partly obtained by private
investment and bankable loans, possibly as much as 1 billion
dollars per year.

Is this amount possible?

This leaves 20 billion dollars to be found in the next decade.
This is a modest goal. Can it be achieved? Are the resources of
the Western nations such that they can give this amount of aid
without suffering serious harm to their own economic systems?
I think it is fair to say that most economists who have studied
this question answer it with an unequivocal "yes"; there is,
however, quite a lot of divergence on *how* it can be done and
indeed there are still, in my opinion, a number of only partly
solved problems in this field.

However, a study of domestic saving and investment on the
part of the richer countries during the fifties (1950–9) gives

[2] Barbara Ward, *India and the West*, Hamish Hamilton, London, 1960,
p. 207.

clear indication that the figure suggested by Paul Hoffman is perfectly possible. In the industrialized countries in this period, gross domestic saving reached an average of 18 per cent to 22 per cent of the gross domestic product (United Kingdom 15·2 per cent, United States 18·6 per cent, Germany 26·3 per cent). This made possible an *increase* of real *per capita* annual income of 2 per cent to 4 per cent in the principal European countries (in the case of Germany 6·9 per cent) and of 1·8 in the United States. In other words, the increase in the standard of living per year for the more developed countries was roughly 3 per cent. Considering that in 1961 according to estimates of Rosenstein-Rodan, the real gross national product *per head* of the United States was 2,790 dollars and 1,472 dollars in Western Europe, while it was only 164 dollars in Africa and 154 dollars in Asia, it should be possible for the 600 million inhabitants of the non-Communist developed countries to devote 2 to 3 billion more from a gross national product reaching nearly 900 billion dollars in order to raise the living standard of the nearly 1½ billion human beings who, though nearly two and a half times as many, have among them a total gross national product of only 200 billion dollars.

If anyone thinks this amount excessive, one may reflect that America has spent nearly 3 billion dollars up to June 1962 (2,700 million to be exact) on equipping a submarine fleet with Polaris missiles alone, quite a small part of her armament and space research programme.

Will it be forthcoming?

The next question to be asked is: will this happen? Will aid of the magnitude necessary be forthcoming? The best way to answer these questions is to consider the factors which make for a sober optimism.

HOPEFUL SIGNS

Various statistics—from U.N.O. and other sources— indicate, in fact, a steadily increasing volume of aid; economic aid and contributions on behalf of the undeveloped countries have doubled in the course of the last decade. In spite of what I have said about the magnitude of the aid and the meagreness of results, the importance of this aid must not be minimized. This represents a huge effort on the part of the more privileged peoples to help the less privileged, a completely new departure on this scale in the relationships between nations and one that can be reasonably expected to grow during the sixties.

For this reason, Paul Hoffman thinks that his comparatively modest goal may be exceeded:

> I am encouraged in this belief by our experience with the Marshall Plan. It was originally estimated by the European Economic Committee headed by Sir Oliver Franks that approximately $29 billion of assistance would be required to restore industrial and agricultural production in Western Europe to pre-war levels, and that it would take four years to reach that goal. Later the Harriman Committee, of which I was a member, estimated that the job could be done for $17 billion. The actual result was that after only two and a half years of the Marshall Plan the work of reconstruction had gone forward with such will that industrial production in Western Europe had jumped to 40 per cent above the highest pre-war figure, and even in agriculture the West Europeans had registered a 20 per cent gain. In the end, the job of European recovery was accomplished with United States aid of only about $13 billion, of which about $1 billion has since been repaid.
>
> Why did this happen? Because of the tremendous upsurge in the spirit of the European people and the enthusiasm with which they went about their job. Thus once more it was proved that you cannot measure or forecast, by statistical analysis or otherwise, the potentialities of the human spirit.

The rate of economic progress in the developed countries gives reason to hope that these countries will increase their efforts to help the developing countries: indeed this has been proclaimed as a major objective of the Six, the European Common Market. This and other arrangements leading to increased world trade will, one hopes, facilitate trade with the developing nations.

Increased investment and increased pre-investment operations are indeed necessary to speed the development of the low-income countries, but the core of the development process is increased production in the developed and under-developed countries alike, linked through increasing international trade: in other words, an expanding world economy. It is hoped therefore that the European Common Market will have a world outlook, not a parochial one, and will be able to help the under-developed countries to increase and safeguard their trade as well as providing aid in the form of investment for them.

Another encouraging sign is the great amount of bilateral *donations* which now amount to between 2 billion and 2½ billion dollars per year. This is in addition to bilateral public and private loans and investment as part of traditional financing methods. Aid through multilateral operations through the agency of international or inter-governmental institutions or organizations is relatively modest. Of these agencies, the International Bank for Reconstruction and Development (the World Bank) was the first. It was founded in 1946. Then followed the International Finance Corporation (1946) and the International Development Association (I.D.A., 1960).

Alongside these financial bodies the United Nations have set on foot a variety of organizations and programmes for technical assistance, relief and aid and a United Nations Special Fund to provide for projects beyond the scope of other Agencies to under-developed countries. Finally, we have to note regional action such as the Colombo Plan (1950), the Development Fund of the European Economic Community (E.E.C.), the Inter-American Bank (1959), and the "Alliance for Progress" (a project for United States governmental aid to South America of 10 billion dollars over a period of ten years).

These are all signs since the last war of a new work of cooperation among men, of a new look in international relations, of a movement towards international social justice on the level of economics.

Paul Hoffman has suggested that at least half of the extra 20 billion dollars to be raised over the next ten years should be administered by the international agencies such as I.D.A.

This latter institution with its emphasis on loans with longer terms of repayment and lower interest rates than are now available, provides the very kind of instrument needed for carrying out this type of international investment. It will not be dominated by the same need to hedge against all the short-term risks, which at present limits the scope of the World Bank. It will be able to make loans for social projects like training programmes and schools, which pay off heavily, but only in the long run. However, I.D.A. as presently conceived has a major defect; its resources are too small. To do its job, it may need a billion dollars a year—not that amount spread over five years, which is the capitalization currently proposed. Under the I.D.A. Articles of Agreement, the United States is committed to provide 32 per cent of the total. If the I.D.A.'s sights were raised to 1 billion dollars a year, the United States would be investing through it 320 million dollars a year.

Andrew Shonfield has made constructive criticisms of the work of all the United Nations Agencies—his suggestions re I.D.A. come close to Paul Hoffman's—which deserve the close attention of all who see the value of aid channelled in this way. It is obvious that the Agencies need greater preparation and organization for the work they may be called on to do. Perhaps even more safeguards are necessary than even he suggests. His proposals for tightening up the efficiency of control and the avoiding of the position where the developing countries have too much say in the allotting of aid of which they themselves will mainly be the recipients are two essential points. But the first might lead to too much power being placed in comparatively few hands and the latter could cause friction unless tactfully executed.

There does then seem to be a sound basis for sober optimism that much of the economic aid needed in the sixties will be forthcoming for the under-developed countries.

I have dealt deliberately with the question of aid independently of the military expenditure necessitated by the cold war and the local "hot" wars that absorb so much money. All the money, and much more than is needed to transform the underdeveloped countries' economies, would be forthcoming if disarmament came over night. However, it is not good enough to say what would be done if disarmament could be brought about. This is unrealistic. Everyone fervently hopes that disarmament will come one day but economic policies cannot be based on hopes or dreams. These countries need aid whether the great powers renounce the arms race or not. We must wipe out poverty, not explain, no matter how convincingly, why we did not have the opportunity to do so. The march of events, history itself, has no time for alibis. If our civilization crumbles, if we descend into another Dark Ages, made more horrible by technology, excuses will be of little help. We may be dead right, but we will be dead.

The developing countries have their part to play also, as I shall indicate later on. In a partnership, both parties must pull their weight. They must put themselves in a position to be helped. It is not unreasonable to expect them to guarantee the proper use of aid, they must have the welfare of their own people at heart and, just as poor persons in private life, they must avoid luxury. I would suggest that the newly independent African country which is spending 12 per cent of her budget on arms and 12 per cent on promoting a Pan-Africanism which is often bitterly opposed to the West is not making a responsible contribution to the partnership for development which is the condition of progress for the developing countries. And Western nations may feel chary of giving a blank cheque to United Nations when, for example, on African matters the policy of the United Nations often seems to be dictated by the Afro-Asian bloc and the Communist bloc acting together. This is not to say that the poverty of the developing countries should be thrown up at them and be a curb on their liberty of action, nor to suggest that because of our help Afro-Asians should always side with the West. Nevertheless, the feelings and legitimate interests of the donor nations deserve some consideration, and, if men and money are provided to help to raise living standards, there is a duty towards the taxpayers who provided the money and towards the intended beneficiaries that the aid really does reach the right quarters. "And without strings" does not mean, cannot mean, "blank cheque" aid which is fair neither to the donors not to the real would-be recipients.

CHAPTER V

COMMUNISM AND
WORLD POVERTY

However much one may want to dissociate the giving of aid to developing countries from politics and divorce it from the Cold War, the realities of the present and the past decade would make this an escapist attitude.

Aid to the under-developed countries from the Soviet Union and the People's "Democracies" in Europe has special aims and special characteristics which must be taken into account.

THE COMMUNIST ATTITUDE TO AID

Although Lenin in 1916 had made it clear that once his revolution was successful, one of the tasks would be to lend economic and technical aid to the backward peoples, it was not until the death of Stalin in 1953—whose policy ran counter to Lenin's ideas—that the U.S.S.R. began to provide economic aid to developing countries, especially in Asia.

From 1954 onwards the Eastern bloc, by a series of agreements, became important partners in making economic aid and technical assistance available. Most of the assistance comes in the form of direct bilateral, inter-governmental agreements. Unlike the Western countries, even the Soviet's contribution to United Nations technical assistance programmes is really bilateral, not multilateral aid, as its contributions are in non-convertible roubles.

There are certain characteristics worthy of note. These aid agreements are usually signed on the occasion of a political visit by the heads of governments concerned. They are rapidly negotiated, they have many benefits for the undeveloped country, they are ostensibly without political strings (though Yugoslavia in 1958 soon found how genuine this claim was), they are generally low-interest loans, not gifts, there is little concern with the credit-worthiness of the receiving countries and repayment of these low-interest, often long-term, loans may even be in kind.

Often a credit is given for a specific purpose, especially to finance heavy industry, for example, the credit of the 132 million dollars repayable at $2\frac{1}{2}$ per cent in twelve years, to provide machine tools and equipment for the steel mill under construction at Bhilai in India in 1959. Numerous technical personnel from the Eastern bloc were put at the disposal of India for this and 700 skilled Indian technicians and engineers were trained in the Soviet Union. This plant will step up steel production potential in India by 60 per cent. The same sort of combined financial and technical assistance has been granted to the then U.A.R., Afghanistan, Indonesia, Ceylon, Argentina, etc.[1]

There is no doubt that the total annual aid is far greater from the West—and includes gifts as well as loans. It has been estimated that the amount of total annual assistance *put to effective use* may be estimated at about 4·8 billion dollars from the West compared to 200 million in 1957 and less than 500 million per year even now from the Eastern bloc. However, Soviet propaganda and the nature of this aid bring sometimes greater prestige than is obtained by the West from their larger contribution. The gift of one million dollars' worth of wheat is consumed and soon forgotten: a factory built by a one million dollar loan from Russia which becomes the property of the Indian government is something lasting and visible.

[1] Cf. Henri Chambre, "Aid from the East bloc countries to the underdeveloped countries", in *World Justice*, Louvain, Volume II, No. 1, September 1960.

There is not space enough to go into more details about th
Russian contribution to the development of the developin
nations. It is necessary to consider the relationship on a wider
basis.

THE ATTRACTION OF COMMUNISM
FOR DEVELOPING COUNTRIES

While recognizing the fact that Communism is not the
monolithic, single-minded system that it is sometimes errone-
ously made out to be (there is a world of difference obviously
between Communism in comparatively rich countries such as
Czechoslovakia and Russia and the Communism of desperately
poor China), there is no doubt that the broad essentials of it as
a materialistic philosophy aiming at an earthly paradise by
totalitarian methods, with an atheistical and anti-religious
background, to be spread throughout the world, are common
to all its manifestations. Deviation is on forms and methods
rather than on basic principles. If Communism were to aban-
don these, it would cease to be Communism. The messianic
character of Communism, the spreading of a cause which will
bring about an economic millennium is an appealing character-
istic of Communism to those who want a secular purpose in
life. It has also made possible the political aggrandizement of
Russia in a way the tsars only dreamt of; it has enabled the
Russians or Chinese Communists to enslave nations while
they preach against colonialism. Nationalism is a good thing
in Ghana, Cuba, or Iraq or anywhere where it will embarrass
or can be used to embarrass Western powers, but it is bad in
countries like Hungary, some Asian province of the far-flung
Russian Empire, or Tibet.

Lenin was always conscious of the potential benefits to
Communism which could arise from the revolt of colonial
peoples against their masters. He did not foresee the comparatively smooth transfer of power, such as happened in
India and in various other colonies, just as Marx had not
foreseen the transformation of the proletariat into a contented
sector of the affluent society. But Lenin's ideas about colonial

oppression and the threat of colonial economic imperialism have been widely accepted by nationalists in emergent nations and explain their resentment and the apparent lack of gratitude which is sometimes shown, even towards generous and well-intentioned Western aid.

There are three things to be considered in the relationship between Communism, or rather the Communist countries, and the developing countries.

First, the fact that in all their relations with these countries Communism keeps in mind the philosophy and political aspirations of its system. The Communist regards these countries as part of the struggle for the world triumph of Communism and seeks indirectly to achieve dominance over them, to gain them for the Communist ideological empire.

Secondly, although this has not been sufficiently appreciated in the West, Communism, in its historical setting of Russian and Chinese Communism, has a great attraction for the leaders of the emerging nations. These leaders see especially how Russian Communists have achieved, by means of their own efforts, in a comparatively short time, the transition from economic chaos and political subservience to a highly industrialized and powerful state.

Thirdly, even when the leaders of the emerging nations have no time for the Communist ideology or indeed for Russian policies, they are tempted, even when they are politically immature, to play one opponent off against the other, to make the Cold War serve their own ends in their desperate bid to achieve rapid economic and social development.[2]

CLASSES TO WHICH COMMUNISM APPEALS

According to the Communist, there are three revolutionary classes in the newly developing areas which may serve Communism's purposes. There are the poverty-stricken workers, the classical proletariat of Marx, the nationalistic intellectuals

[2] Cf. Barbara Ward, *Rich Nations and Poor Nations*, Hamish Hamilton, London, 1962, Chapter III.

and the peasants suffering from age-old land hunger made more acute by rapidly increasing populations. The Communists hope, by championing the cause of these different groups, to lead all three under the banner of the revolt against colonialism and the new economic imperialism and thus to have the most powerful political and social forces in the world today under their control.

In Asia, South America and Africa, all these three classes of people are represented in varying degrees and in different parts. Land hunger is most prevalent in South America and Asia, especially in Indonesia, where there are large Communist parties. Indonesia, for example, has a Communist party with 2,000,000 members. Nationalism is the more powerful factor in Africa, and among the leaders of the African emerging nations are those who look towards Moscow for their inspiration if not for their orders.

But in all three continents, Communist support is based upon protests against hardships or injustices, suffered or observed. Because they have no backlog of colonial rule, with its history of exploitation as well as its more recent beneficial and positive achievements, the Communists win ready acceptance for their own propaganda assertions that they help poor struggling peoples to win their freedom from colonial rule, and that they fight for the improvement of the lot of the poor and under-privileged. In spite of their European record, and long years of domestic oppression, they somehow give the impression that only the Communists care and even the aid that the West gives in far greater abundance than the Communist world is smeared. As Christopher Hollis has said, the Western nations dare not look over the hedge, while the Russians can steal the horse and get away with it. The impression is given that the only interest of the free world in Asia, Africa and Latin America is a vested, Cold War one, inspired only by military and political considerations, whereas the Communist interest grows straight out of their beliefs and is therefore genuine. Taking a limited local view, limited in time also, this impression often seems justified to the people of a particular country. The Communists often seem to be the only ones that are doing things about the undoubted injustices and oppressions which exist.

But when one considers the Communist policy throughout the world, the actions and motivations of the different Communist parties in the various geographical and political set-ups, then a common theme runs through their actions. Communists are interested in agitation not in aid. Their political motivation and purpose are quite different from those of the people in a given developing area. They spring from the Communists' firmly-held belief that the existing social system, whatever it may be, must first be destroyed if a Communist one is to be built. Quite naturally it is Communism which is the Communists' aim. It is this, therefore, for which they work and fight and to this cause they subordinate all else. Their activities should not be confused with the real fight for social justice. But they realize, as the leaders of the Bolshevik revolution did, that people will struggle and die for the ordinary things of life, things which should be the birthright of every man, provided also there is a direct and simple appeal to justice and idealism. The Communists who brought about the successful Russian revolution did not preach Marxism. The slogan under which the revolution was fought had nothing to do with Communism, but a great deal to do with social justice and the most urgent needs of the common people. It was "Bread, land, peace and homes" and that is the same message which they are bringing to the under-developed countries today, and it is by means of this that they hope to achieve power as they did over forty years ago in Russia.

It is only before and during the revolution that the Communist makes himself the great fighter against social and racial injustice and the champion of international social justice. He is concerned with revolution, not with reform, but agitation for reforms can serve the cause of revolution. Every injustice therefore adds grist to his mill, provided that he never loses sight of his main goal. Lenin told Communists everywhere that they must be interested in reforms only in so far as these might be used for the revolution. The Communist, he said, will accept reform in order to use it as a means wherewith to link legal work with illegal work, in order to use it as a screen behind which his illegal activities for the revolutionary preparation of the masses for the overthrow of the bourgeoisie may be intensified. This is what the revolutionary utilization of reforms and agreements in imperialistic empires means, according to Lenin, and Stalin called reforms "stepping stones to revolutions".

This may strike the non-Communist as grossly immoral, even inhuman. The well-trained Communist does not see it this way. He believes that a Communist world would be the best of all possible worlds and to achieve this end he must be prepared to use any methods which will serve his Communist ends, and he has his own views on morality as on everything else. He takes as his only guide Lenin's maxim that morality must be subordinated wholly to the interests of class struggle. Communist campaigns in Asian, African and Latin American cities on such questions as food, housing, and social conditions are therefore not directly inspired by moral indignation at the existence of preventable evils, nor by the determination to end them. They spring from the desire to destroy capitalism and put Communism in its place. It does not mean, of course, that the Communist as an individual never feels the same compassion as other men but his Marxism tells him that it will not be by compassion that the masses will be helped, but by bitter class struggle. Communist papers everywhere follow the same pattern of bitterly and remorselessly exposing bad social conditions, inadequate housing, low wages and so on, but there are no calls to help which stem from an understanding of those who have to endure these evils. The call is for those concerned to *struggle* against them. Again it is agitation not aid. Injustices are spotlighted not in order to be remedied, to be *fought* against. Moreover, only those issues which can be used in this way are featured. There is no attempt to build up a public opinion against injustice as such.

The attempts of the Western world to aid the under-developed countries are not welcomed even grudgingly as a means of relieving the unhappy lot of the under-privileged. Rather they are opposed and sneered at. An example of this is the Point Four Programme work in Persia in 1953 and 1954 which met active opposition from Communist sources but which achieved a good measure of success in spite of this. The United Nations Organizations such as W.H.O., F.A.O. and U.N.E.S.C.O. get little support from the Eastern bloc. They are interested in revolution not assistance unless aid can be used to serve their purposes.

Their aim is to create disorder as their various activities in India, for example, show. Just as in the Communist revolution itself, the slogan under which the revolution was fought had nothing to do with Communism but a great deal to do with social justice and the most urgent needs of the common people, so in the developing countries they realize that while it is impossible to achieve current political aims of Communists by purely political means, it is often relatively easy, as was the case in Castro's Cuba, to achieve these same ends by exploiting economic issues. The distinction between the Christian and humanist agitation for social justice and Communist agitation is that the former is aiming for social reforms while the Communists are aiming at revolution and the destruction of the social system so that it can be replaced by one which will be based upon the ending of all private ownership in the means of production, including land.[3]

Since 1957, when Khrushchev assumed power, very much more aid, often in kind, often involving big economic and industrial missions and infiltration of Communist advisers, has been given. It is noteworthy that the Communists themselves hold studiously aloof from the aid and help given by the United Nations Organizations which have been helping to make people aware of the iniquity of the immense growing inequalities between nations and which have tried, however imperfectly,

[3] Cf. Douglas Hyde, "Injustice and Communism", *World Justice*, Louvain, Vol. 1, No. 2, Dec. 1959.

to find remedies by means of money and technical assistance to remedy them.

The genuine nationalist when engaging in activity against a colonial power does things for one reason, the Communist for another and quite a different one. By leading the anti-colonial struggle the Communist hopes to remain in the saddle after the colonies have been freed, and at the same time to weaken the imperialist countries of the West by means of costly and protracted colonial wars. The scope for such intervention, of course, has been weakened very much by the granting of independence to these nations but there is still scope for fishing in the troubled waters of political rivalries and economic weakness, the aftermath of the struggle for independence, and for filling the vacuum all too often left by the departure of former colonial powers.

It is significant that, in the Philippines and other parts of the world where drastic action has been taken and has been seen to be taken against land hunger and other social injustices freely by democratic means, the power of the Communist party has dwindled. That is what the Western world must realize. It is no use fighting Communists by guns or by direct means while all the abuses which throw open temptations to Communism remain. So long as there is such great need for reform of land systems in South America and Asia, so long will the attractions of the Communist party remain strong, even though it may be driven underground. Communism can only be fought indirectly by doing what is right, what is in keeping with the principles of Catholic international social justice.

COMMUNIST MATERIALISM

But there is another element that I have indicated which makes Communism attractive to the leaders of newly independent countries. There is a materialism in the West which is being absorbed by the East and also by most African nations.

In its best form it could indeed be embraced and ennobled by Christian principles. For this materialism expresses itself in enormous interest in the natural order and in a determined attempt to penetrate its secrets by means of science and it is committed to the possibility of better conditions on earth, in a belief that man has the right, even a duty, to improve material conditions both for himself and for his fellow men. There is nothing inimical to the best Christian thought in this materialism so long as it stops there, but Communism attempts to make materialism the measure and basis of all things. This strange transformation of materialism into a kind of religion gives power to the Communist dream of a world made one and equal and rich, which has a powerful appeal to the élite and the intelligentsia of a developing country, even though this ideal may not have been achieved, indeed may have been shelved in Communist ruled countries. The idea too, of equality, "from each according to his capacities, to each according to his needs", is a doctrine which appeals to those who believe they are suffering from international social inequality—the underprivileged nations.

Perhaps the most attractive aspect of Communism to them, which to us may seem its least attractive feature, is the forceful accumulation of capital which has led to the highly developed, if uneven, industrialized economy of Soviet Russia. Soviet Russia is a model of what can be done by a country which started as many of the emerging countries are starting, far behind in the race for economic progress. Stalin built up this economy not by destroying capitalism, but by destroying private capitalism and by introducing a state capitalism which used far more rugged methods than the early capitalist system in Britain dared to use. Even in a normally prosperous country between 10 and 15 per cent of savings is regarded as a pretty high figure, and for poor countries, although such savings may be necessary according to economic theory, they are extremely high, too high, unless helped by economic aid from the more developed countries. But the Russian plan drove the figure up to 25 and 30 per cent of the national income and these massive savings poured into the new industries, into the new developments beyond the Urals, and into the vast expansion of mines and transport and education and research. It came from the people as it could come from no other source.

The partial success of Stalin has blinded people to the immense wholesale and ruthlessly inflicted sufferings of the thirties. Indeed there are some of quite liberal tendencies in the West, as I have suggested, who almost feel inclined to say now that it was worth the price and that if a nation is to become industrialized perhaps a short, sharp agony inflicted by policies such as Stalin's might be even preferable to the long-drawn-out social injustice of the nineteenth century. This paradox of liberals, in their dislike of abuses of capitalism being prepared to accept the even greater abuses of Communist régimes for the sake of the good achieved, is only explicable on this assumption. Forced growth achieved through the central planning power of an autocratic state has an appeal to countries caught in the half-way land between the need for change and the capacity to change in fact.

We must never forget that in the developing countries the ideal of free democracy is of relatively late growth and has not really touched the lives of the people. As an Indian said: "We are more interested in food than in freedom." How can the blithe promises of independence be achieved when all around the institutions and inhibitions of the old static society seem to remain more or less intact? It is in this mood of frustration that Communism can speak. It attacks the traditional leaders of society, the old rulers and princes, the old landlords, the entrenched groups in industry and commerce, the men who seem to stand in the way of the emergence of the new forces of modernism. Communism attacks foreign control, it denounces imperialism. In the economic field, it offers an intense discipline and saving by compelling people to postpone consumption. It attacks head-on the most difficult task in any society where people live so near the margin of absolute poverty that saving must be an agonizing choice. By removing choice and compelling accumulation, Communism offers a pattern of quick growth. The fundamental strategic claim is enhanced by other advantages. Communism has been shown to be a method of seizing power and developing a society through the work of a small élite, a small group of people. In most of the under-developed areas the number of men and women who feel themselves able, educated and dedicated enough to undertake the making of the new society is necessarily small. This attraction is reinforced by a certain bold simplicity: Marx's determination to explain everything in terms of his revolution. The appeal of a firm and simple explanation is intense to confused leaders of newly-freed nations facing immense problems. There is a fascination in the Communist propaganda which claims to have the prescription for the future, and can point to what they have already done by their own efforts without outside aid.

THE NEED FOR A POSITIVE POLICY OF COMMITMENT ON THE PART OF THE WEST

The Communists say that they have all the answers; we in the West are not so certain. This is so not because we are not concerned, not because we have not got the interest, but because the problems themselves are so complex. We do not dare to be dogmatic yet dogmatism has its attractions. We cannot be definite even, because we have not got a clear programme, decisively expressed, to offer the under-developed countries. We have not got even a very clear understanding of their rights and duties or our own in helping them.[4]

This is also due to the fact that there is little sense of urgency about the developing areas. There is not a policy of high priority to help emerging nations. There is still too much concern with purely domestic issues or with the problems of armaments and the Cold War, while aid is piecemeal and haphazard. No-one expects clear panaceas which do not often stand up to the cold light of reality or which can only be achieved at the expense of an even greater amount of human suffering which exists in the under-developed world today.

But we do need to study and act on the best we can do to aid

[4] Cf. Barbara Ward, *Rich Nations and Poor Nations*, Chapter III.

these countries. This best, which is a compound of solutions derived from a consideration of the complexity of the subject, may not be perfect, but it would be adequate if it was acted on wholeheartedly by the nations of the West with as much conviction as it is proposed by those thinkers who have given their best attention to the subject; in other words, if the plans which have been produced and suggested by people such as Paul Hoffman, Barbara Ward, Andrew Shonfield, Professor Tinbergen and others are not dismissed as visionary but are taken as the absolute minimum necessary for our commitment to the under-developed countries. We may make mistakes, we may not solve all the problems, but it would be seen by the whole world that we are committed to their solution in a spirit of partnership, in a spirit of Christian understanding and compassion. If South America were to adopt land reform policies of far-reaching consequences, financed by America and by the Western nations, the ground would be cut from under Communism and the negative approach would lose its force before the positive dynamism of the developed and under-developed countries acting in concert for the benefit of the poorer half of mankind.

We need faith and hope in ourselves, we need to forget the many and real excuses we have for not helping the other countries. It is true that if suddenly disarmament became a fact a huge amount of money and material and technical know-how would be available. As President Kennedy pointed out on his Telstar press interview towards the end of July 1962: "We could balance our budget tomorrow if it were not for our defence commitments and our aid to the under-developed countries." All those things are true but they are alibis. We have all the technical knowledge, we have all the material resources, we have all the financial potential to wipe poverty off the face of this earth in this generation or in this century at least. What is lacking is a sense of urgency, a sense of optimism, a conviction that we can and must do it.

But for this revolution of ideas, we need more than an empty and negative opposition to Communism. It would be a bad thing if Communism were to triumph throughout the world. But it would be equally bad if we were to aid the under-developed countries merely to stop Communism triumphing. What is needed is a clear statement of the principles which should drive the richer countries to help the poorer; dynamic ideas which could make the Western nations emerge from their closed-in world of ever-increasing affluence guarded by ever-increasing armaments of ever-increasing destructive power.

The social teaching of the Church has the principles which would lead to a manifesto of more far-reaching importance than that of Karl Marx. These principles are mainly based on the natural law and can easily be accepted by those who do not share belief in the doctrines of the Church.

To the religious zeal of the Communists needs to be opposed the dedicated commitment of Christian men and women and of all those who, belonging to no religion, still respect the Christian heritage of the West, sure of the basis of their position and resolved to translate Christian principles into their every-day work of ensuring that sufficient money, material, technical aid and education should be available to enable the developing countries to rise out of the slough of hunger and poverty. Let us make no mistake about it, this is the challenge, the central task, the most explosive problem of the twentieth century. On the solution of this problem depends the peace of the world far more than on the possession of the hydrogen bomb or efforts to "contain" Communism. Communism would wither and die—as some of its more extreme doctrinaire tenets have done in Soviet Russia—if the abuses and injustices on which it feeds faded away. Peace is the fruit of justice and charity, not of the deadlock of two great powers poised for war but afraid to embark on it.

Lord Boyd Orr nearly ten years ago clearly saw this. He said:

> The Western powers are faced with the rising waves of revolt of Asia, Africa and Latin America against poverty. They can try and resist it by force or try and buy it off by the offer of technical assistance and trifling loans with political strings attached to them

which will break on the first strain. In that case, they will ultimately be destroyed or submerged. On the other hand, either with or without the cooperation of the U.S.S.R., they could recognize the inevitable and use their overwhelming industrial superiority to create a world of plenty. In so doing, they would gain a new power and prestige by assuming leadership in the march of the human family to the new age of peace and prosperity and the common brotherhood of man, which modern science has made the only alternative to the decline and fall of the Western civilization.

CHAPTER VI

THE CHURCH'S TEACHING ON INTERNATIONAL SOCIAL JUSTICE

World poverty exists on a large scale. There are millions, hundreds of millions of our fellow human beings who live lives out of keeping with their dignity as human beings and children of our heavenly Father. As we have seen, it is possible to remedy this state of affairs, to wipe poverty off the face of the earth in this century. To do so, as we have also seen, will require great efforts and possibly considerable sacrifices on the part of the richer nations who will have to make large sums available for the development of the developing countries.

The rich have always been allergic to helping the poor, they have always been able to find excuses for not doing so. In the last century many Christians salved their consciences with the thought, a blasphemous twist to our Lord's words, that the poor are always with us; that they are a different kind of being, that they would not profit by their conditions being improved. They are naturally lazy or indolent or apathetic and that is why they are poor; that somehow or other they have not got the same feelings, the same aspirations, as their richer brethren, so one need not bother with them too much. Or, without going so far as that, one might have indeed had pity and compassion for them but, following the economic theory of the day, one would have just shrugged one's shoulders and lamented that there was nothing one could do about it, except perhaps a certain amount of soup-kitchen aid, when poverty became too oppressive and starvation was round the corner.

We hear quite a number of similar excuses for not helping the under-developed countries even nowadays. Most people, when they become aware of the problems, pay lip service to the need to help the under-developed countries but like the rich man they find any number of excuses for not doing so. Nations have commitments, they have balance of payment problems, they have defence problems. These are allowed to make nonsense of the calculations of economists that the amount of aid needed to help the under-developed countries could easily be raised not by taking away from the standard of living of the developed countries, not by interfering with their riches, but merely by devoting to this 1 per cent of the 4 per cent annual *increase* in the *per capita* income of the Western nations. When economists make this kind of calculation, it seems extremely easy for the developed countries to provide all the aid that is necessary. But when one does come down to concrete realities, as Andrew Shonfield has said, "The balance of payments makes skinflints of us all", and where thousands of millions were shown to be possible, a few millions are refused.

It is not possible to solve this problem on the basis of pure charity, nor is moral indignation a sufficient substitute for economic know-how. So some of the excuses of the rich nations in the present economic set-up have their validity. For example, it would cause a great economic upheaval if all the surplus food produce, for example the farm produce of the United States, were suddenly dumped on the world market. A balance of payments crisis, the sort of crisis we are becoming used to in America or Britain, sparking off a possible recession, would be no help to the under-developed countries. They have bitter memories of what a world depression can do to them when the American depression of 1957 and its resulting impact on world prices caused a slump in the prices of primary commodities on which many of the under-developed countries depend; so much so, indeed, that the value of loans by the World Bank over six years were wiped out by the loss to the under-developed countries caused by the fall in the prices which they got for their products.

Nevertheless, if it can be shown that help to the under-developed countries is a duty of justice and charity, this will give urgency to the consideration, to the planning, which could lead to massive help being given within the framework of the present world economy, or would even lead to changes in the structure of the world economic system.

Under the pressure of war, superhuman things are done. Things which in peace-time are completely impossible, or are regarded as such, become the normal thing. We are still bogged down by the difficulties of using atomic energy for peaceful uses. It took only three years for the atomic bomb to be developed when there was the urgent war need for it to be developed. The fantastic difficulties to be overcome in order to put men into space overawe the average layman while the colossal sums devoted to space travel vie with the huge expenditure on armaments.[1] Until a few years ago, most people thought space travel a wild dream of sensational fiction writers. But the difficulties were overcome, the problems solved. Why? Because men *wanted* to achieve this goal sufficiently and were given the capital to make their dreams possible by their incredible God-given ingenuity. The conclusion that men, at present, do not want enough the revolution in living standards for poorer countries is inescapable. Lester Pearson's bitter aphorism "we prepare for war like precocious giants and for peace like retarded pigmies" will not be proved untrue overnight. It will come as the result of ideas, the same as every revolution has come, the same as Communism came. It will come as the result of a revolution of ideas, but a revolution not based on negative destruction, but based on the ideals of justice which appeal to all men of good will.

---

[1] Forty billion dollars (£14,282 m.) have been voted by the U.S. senate to put three men on the moon by 1970.

THE RÔLE OF CATHOLIC SOCIAL PRINCIPLES

The Catholic Church has a sane coherent doctrine of international social justice. It is true that it is not worked out in all its details because the subject is a comparatively new one,[2] and until recently there was a very natural and very necessary concern with social justice within the nation. Still there are some fundamental principles enunciated by the popes that would be acceptable, I think to almost all men of good will, of whatever religious creed they belong, or even if they do not accept any religious allegiance, which could have a powerful impact on thought in this field.

All men have a right to a living

All men by the very fact that they are men have a right to the use of sufficient earthly goods, as to enable them to support and develop life in accordance with the demands of human dignity. All men have this right. Pius XII defined this right and stressed that one of the main reasons for so-called over-population is neglect of this principle.[3] He emphasized that there must be a more just distribution of the world's resources so that all men may have the minimum share, at least, of earthly goods to which their nature and the will of God entitles them. He pointed out the fundamental point of the social question is this, "that the goods created by God for all men should in the same way reach all men . . . justice guiding and charity helping. . . . God does not wish that some should have exaggerated riches while others are in such straits that they lack the bare necessities of life." The pope derived this basic right from the nature of man; he further declared, "that this is not a right which in any way can be overridden even by other clear rights because this right is absolutely fundamental".

[2] Even *The Church and Social Justice*, by J.-Y. Calvez and J. Perrin, the recently published synthesis of eighty years of the Church's social teaching has little reference to it.

[3] Cf. A. Zimmerman, S.V.D., *Overpopulation: A Study of Papal Teachings*, Catholic University of Washington Press, Washington D.C., 1957, pp. 73 f.

The right to private property, for example, and the rights of the state are derived from natural law and as such they are from God. However, they are *subordinate to* and indeed are meant to help men fulfil their basic right of natural justice which says that all men have a claim to at least that minimum share in the goods of the earth which will enable them to live a life in keeping with their human needs and dignity as men. The same pope condemned the glaring discrepancy between the standards of living in different countries. He said that this is against justice, charity and prudence. Justice demands that the goods intended by God for all his creatures should be so fairly distributed among nations that all have an adequate supply of goods and services. Nations which have an abundance of goods have a duty to share them amongst those who are disproportionately poor. Charity demands that peoples of the family of nations should assist each other, and prudence dictates that we should not wantonly try each other's patience by perpetuating a system of glaring inequalities in living standards; otherwise a burning resentment will arise which will explode in new wars.

Aid must be effective and sufficient

The aid which the richer countries owe the poor must be governed itself by certain principles. The most obvious of these is effectiveness. To fulfil an obligation of the magnitude which faces these nations, it is not sufficient to give comparatively trifling sums or make insufficient, insignificant sacrifices of national income. Aid must be proportioned to the need. Only massive assistance is effective in face of the massive proportions of the problem of half the world being at, or near, subsistence level.

The danger of glaring inequalities

Pius XII throughout his pontificate showed great concern for the poorer nations of the world, and the growing inequalities which existed between nations, from the very first days of his pontificate; he spoke out about the problems of the undeveloped countries and even during the war, when nations were fighting for survival, he kept reminding them of their duties which would be a guarantee of peace. For example, in 1939 he said: "Justice requires that all men acknowledge and defend the rights of human freedom and human dignity, and *that the infinite wealth and resources with which God has endowed* the whole earth shall be distributed in conformity with right reason for the use of his children."

And in the middle of the war in his Christmas message of 1942 he said that he who would have the star of peace shine out and stand over society should show respect for a practical realization of the following fundamental personal rights: ". . . the right in principle to marry and achieve the aim of married life, the right to conjugal and domestic society."

This right to marry and have children is also a fundamental right, as fundamental as the right of every man to at least a minimum standard of living in keeping with his human dignity. So when the bogey of over-population was raised, although the pope realized the difficulties, he was against those who saw birth control, or unwise population policies based on it, as a panacea for world poverty, as if numbers alone caused hunger and want. In 1952 he said:

> Certainly we would not deny that this or that region is at present burdened by a relatively excessive population, but the desire to solve the difficulty with a formula that a number of its inhabitants should be regulated according to the public economy is equivalent to subvert the order of nature and the entire psychological and moral world which is bound up with it. What an error it would be to blame the natural order for the present miseries when it is clear that these derive from the lack of mutual solidarity of men and peoples.

The pope stressed the intense interest of the Church in social and economic affairs and linked this with her concern for the eternal welfare of souls. Bad living conditions tend to make a healthy spiritual life impossible. There is the other extreme of excessive wealth and greed which has the same effect; both are to be avoided. When our Lord said, "Blessed are the poor in spirit" he did not mean that people should live in destitution. Pius XII was well aware of this when he said: "The normal growth and increase of religious life presupposes a certain measure of healthy economic conditions. Who can resist a pang of emotion on seeing how economic misery and social evil make a Christian life according to the commands of God more difficult, and too often demand heroic sacrifices?"

Hardly a year passed without some wise and profound utterance on some aspect of the complicated situation. He dealt with international trade, emigration, capital assistance, technical assistance, the use of technology in solving economic problems and many other ways of positively coping with problems of raising the living standards of the poorer half of the world.

Pope John XXIII's concern for the poor and hungry

From the time of his accession in 1958 Pope John XXIII manifested the same solicitude as his predecessor for the poor and the hungry and he showed great interest in organizations whose aim it was to promote the well-being of the hungry millions. In May 1960, he welcomed the delegates to the conference organized by The Food and Agricultural Organization to prepare for The Freedom from Hunger Campaign with these words:

> You have come for the pope's blessing on a vast enterprise, which is now engaging your energies and attention, the organization on a world-wide scale of the Campaign Against Hunger recently launched by the Director-General of the Food and Agriculture Organizations of the United Nations. You are welcome, for your aims coincide with those of the Church in this matter and the task on which you are engaged seems supremely deserving of our approbation and encouragement. What, in fact, is the Church's task on earth? It is to continue the work of Christ, and it is written of him that "He went about doing good and healing . . ." (Acts 10. 38). He also warmly recommended to his followers the spiritual and corporal works of mercy, and the first on the list of these latter is "to feed the hungry". . . .

But you also are sensible, after the example of Christ, of a feeling of deep compassion for the innumerable multitudes of men—more than half the human race—who are undernourished. It will require an immense collective effort to raise them out of their miserable state and to place within their reach an intellectual and moral life more worthy of man and more in keeping with the will of God [Having paid tribute to the immense achievements of F.A.O., the pope went on to speak of what remained to be done:] An enormous amount still remains to be done. The first task is to bring to the attention of the entire world—if this can be done— the sad problem of hunger and undernourishment. This is the first objective of the campaign to which your organizations are applying their intelligence and efforts.

Millions of human beings suffer from hunger; others, while they do not, strictly speaking, go hungry, are underfed. These are the facts. They must be made known, they must be preached from the house-tops, as the Gospel advises: "Preach ye on the house-tops" (Matt. 10. 27). Consciences must be awakened to a sense of the responsibility that rests on the human community and on each individual, on the most privileged people especially. Nobody can nowadays offer the excuse, in a world where distances count for nothing, that he is unaware of the needs of his far-away brother, or that it is not his job to help him. We are all collectively responsible for the undernourished. That is the conviction which your organizations are going to assist in spreading through public opinion, which—once it has been aware of the facts—will demand appropriate measures and will give its support to their execution. . . .

Thus we are confident that, in giving our fullest encouragement to you, our words will travel beyond our present audience and will reach all our sons throughout the world, will reach all men of good-will as a pressing invitation to take part in this great charitable movement, this immense "work of mercy" which the "Campaign against Hunger" is to be. And it is with all our heart that we invoke on all who take part in it—whether as individuals or collectively—and in particular on yourselves and your organizations, the choicest blessings of the all-powerful and merciful God.

MATER ET MAGISTRA

International social justice

On May 15th, 1961 Pope John XXIII issued the Encyclical *Mater et Magistra* which was intended as a successor to *Rerum Novarum* and *Quadragesimo Anno* and had for its aim the christianizing of the social order. Much of what the pope says has relevance mainly for the developed countries. But one part of the Encyclical, Part III, "New Aspects of the Social Question" has a section devoted exclusively to the needs of the developing countries. It has the title—a significant one—"The Demands of Justice in the Relationship between Nations of Differing Economic Development." In this section Pope John summarizes all that his predecessor, and he himself has said on the subject of international social justice. This section applies Catholic social principles to the relationship between nations, although the pope does not develop, as *Rerum Novarum* and *Quadragesimo Anno* did, *ideas* of social justice but treats largely of its practice.

Rerum Novarum was called "The Workers' Charter" because it dealt with the great changes brought about by the industrial revolution which had mainly acted against the interest of the working class, so that this class was an immensely depressed sector of the economic life within nations. *Quadragesimo Anno* dealt with the breakdown of *laissez-faire* capitalism after World War I. Both Encyclicals concentrated on the nation-state as the economic unit treating international issues only in so far as they affected the nation. *Mater et Magistra* is the first Encyclical to deal with social justice between nations. It was natural that Leo XIII and Pius XII should treat the social question with regard to the more limited area of nation-states. Until this century economic units had always been limited and in any case the needs within the nation were so great that i t was obviously good to put the nation's own house in order before looking outside. In this century, each country has come to be considered responsible for its own social problems. This was one of the great achievements of the Encyclical *Rerum Novarum* (though of course other factors contributed to bring this about) because until its publication this sense of social responsibility within the nation was ill developed in the states of the nineteenth century.

Rerum Novarum ushered in a change largely in industrial relations which brought about a new concept of social justice, the fruit of a conviction that something should and could be done to give every member of the community the opportunity to lead a fully human life.

The implications of social justice were institutionalized in social legislation; trade unions, for example, were given legal standing and social security measures were enacted. Within this framework industrial relations were raised from the law of the jungle to the level of a community concern.

But even when the idea of social responsibility on a national scale had begun to develop, it still was a far cry from responsibility for the problems of another nation. It was taken for granted that certain nations were poor, were undeveloped. It might well be that personal charity was moved by some disaster such as flood or famine to make people feel a momentary concern and even to contribute generously to help another country in misfortune. But the idea of international social justice—social justice between nations—was hardly applied. The idea that social distributive justice should supplement commutative justice within nations and by its claims make every member of the community responsible for the well-being of every other member had gained ground by World War II and was intensively applied after it. But it is only slowly, since the end of World War II, that this idea of international social justice has grown. The idea of a social justice relationship between nations, justice governing the international community, is still embryonic. But within the last two decades there has been a remarkable change among farsighted thinkers and statesmen and within the past few years this change has become increasingly extended to ordinary thinking members of the community in the richer countries.

Pius XII was a leading pioneer in developing and urging this concept of international social justice, as we have seen. In many addresses he emphasized the essential oneness of mankind and the consequent, mutual responsibility of the members of this single human family. He made constant appeals for the stripping away of artificial barriers whether of race or nations or economics, so that a stable world order supported by international social justice might emerge. Today, although this sense of the international social community is still feeble, the whole moral climate is different. This has been due in many cases to the breaking down of barriers of distance and time which the War began. Soldiers from the richer countries fought all over the world and many soldiers from the less developed countries travelled extensively and had opportunities to see the power and riches that technological progress had brought to the West. Communications, mass communication media and travel, have annihilated distance and have brought home as never before the reality of the division of the world into "haves" and "have-nots". For better or worse the world is becoming, indeed to a large extent has become, a single economic unity. Not only that, but the Christian Church itself since the beginning of this century, and especially in the last twenty or thirty years has developed wider horizons. The reasons for this are clear if one considers, for example, that the Catholic population of Africa has increased fourteen-fold since the year 1900—that Africa is a more Catholic country than England. In his Christmas message of 1945, Pius XII stressed this when he said:

> In former times the life of the Church in its visible aspect deployed its strength preferably in the countries of Europe from which it spread out like a majestic river to what may be called the periphery of the world.
> Today on the contrary, it is manifested as an exchange of life and energy between all the members of Christ's mystical body on earth. Many countries in other continents have long since passed

beyond the missionary stage in their ecclesiastical organizations: they are governed by their own hierarchy and they contribute spiritually and materially to the whole Church, whereas formerly they did nothing but receive.

The motives which have brought about the one world of economists have been largely materialistic and secular but their achievements have been no less real for that and it would be naive and unrealistic to refuse to accept this fact. As Dr Sen pointed out in 1960, in the past two decades great upheavals have swept the world as much in the political and social field as in the scientific and technological spheres, they have contributed to form ideas and aspirations and fundamentally altered our vision of the future.

Today, the world has suddenly become one, in a way it never was before. Everywhere men are talking about the undeveloped countries and more far-sighted statesmen are seeing the first object of policy must be to raise the standards of living of the undeveloped nations.

Where men were once worried about the industrial worker, they now worry about the agricultural worker and the small farmer and landless peasant, especially in the undeveloped countries of the world. The times clearly demanded some authoritative word from Rome on farm problems; and on a world divided between rich and poor nations, in which the rich are growing richer and the poor are growing poorer; with the complication that poorer populations on the whole are increasing very much more rapidly than those of the more favoured nations, and this fact is aggravating a problem of poverty and want which is already extremely formidable.

Part III of *Mater et Magistra* responds to the realities of the international scene in the beginning of the second decade of the second half of the twentieth century just as *Rerum Novarum* and *Quadragesimo Anno* reacted to the situations at the time of their publication. Before going on to consider in detail the

---

[4] Quoted by Christopher Hollis in *The Church and Economics* in this series.

contents of *Mater et Magistra*, it may be well to reflect on the urgency of the present situation. *Rerum Novarum* in some ways, although a masterly document, brilliantly summarizing and even pioneering the social doctrine of the Church, was a failure, or at least only partially successful, because it was not acted on rapidly and efficiently enough to bring about the transformation of society which would have saved the working class, or large numbers of it, from defection from the Church, and which would have prevented the rise of Communism.

This is no criticism of the marvellous work of Leo XIII since 1878 which culminated in *Rerum Novarum*, because even when he issued his Encyclical, it was ahead of its time and was regarded almost with horror in conservative circles.

Today we face the same situation on the international level, with regard to the poor peoples of the world, as faced individual countries with regard to their proletariat a hundred years ago. Disraeli wrote of the 'two nations' in Victorian England, the rich and the poor. It is worth reflecting that if Karl Marx had found social justice in Victorian England, *Christian* Victorian England and other countries in the nineteenth century, *Das Kapital* would never have been written and we would not have a world with one-quarter of its population under effective Communist control and one-third under Communist influence. Although we must aid the people of the under-developed countries because it is right to do so, it would be naive to forget that if we do not call them brothers, others will call them comrades.

What I have just said about the climate of opinion in the present situation gives hope that the majestic statements of Pope John XXIII will be acted on more rapidly and with far greater success in preventing the defection of nations, and there are signs that it is already doing so.

The pope and agriculture

In the introduction to Part III of the *Mater et Magistra*— "Changes in the Social Question"—the new factor of the widening of the social horizon is stressed by the pope and he insists that the principles of justice and equity which had been set forth by his predecessors and which applied chiefly to the relationship between working men and their employers has now to be extended to different economic sectors, developing areas, and even different countries in different stages of economic development. There follows a detailed treatment of agriculture as the weak sector in the economic life of nations. The pope does not differentiate in this section between developed and under-developed nations. But the relevance of his words to the developing countries is obvious.

As Dr Sen has so wisely said, the ultimate solution to the problems of poverty must be sought in an integrated approach to balanced development of developing countries. It should be recognised that agriculture is the key sector in such development. Sixty to eighty per cent of the people of under-developed countries derive their livelihood from the land. Agriculture must provide food for the people and a margin to start a process of capital formation. It is essential therefore that the initial impulse to improve production should come from improvement in this sector.

The pope noted the exodus from the rural regions to urban centres which is occurring on a large scale in all countries, especially in some developing nations, and which is creating problems difficult to solve. As industry develops and technology advances, some shifts of this kind are to be expected, but the reason why they are taking place on such a large scale cannot be attributed solely to this type of progress. It is due also to other factors, including the vital one that almost everywhere agriculture is a depressed sector within the economy. As a result, nations are greatly concerned with narrowing the imbalance in productive efficiency between agriculture and industry, with reducing the difference between rural and other living standards and with cancelling the inferiority complex which farmers have come to feel about their work. (Not much progress on these lines has been made in the less-developed countries.)

It is not unreasonable to suppose that the enthusiasm with which the pope writes in this sector is due to his own rural upbringing and to his appreciation of the value of the life of a farmer to the community, not only by his contribution to the feeding of it, but also because of the virtues which farming life seems to favour. The pope gives a beautiful description of the vocation and mission of farm life. He also gives a number of wise directives to raise the status of agriculture and the agricultural worker, but he is aware that his words on the vocation and dignity of farming must seem a mockery to many of the downtrodden peasants of under-developed countries, whose way of life in the words of Hobbes may well be described "nasty, brutish and short". So it is a natural transition from this part of the Encyclical to the lengthy section dealing with the relationships between the developing and the developed countries of the world which, significantly, the pope puts under the heading of justice.

The demands of justice between nations

An agricultural and economic revolution is needed in these countries as we have shown. It is one which economists easily prove to us to be completely impossible without help from the developed nations as we have seen. Unlike Pius XII, Pope John XXIII spends little time *in proving* the duty of aiding the under-developed countries. He takes it for granted as flowing from the principle of the solidarity of all nations. He is more concerned in the way this aid should be given; so that it should be effective, positive, efficient and joined to scientific and technical assistance, and that it should avoid the harmful effect that such aid, motivated by the wrong reasons or given in the wrong ways, might have:

> Probably the most difficult problem today concerns the relationship between political communities which are economically advanced and those which are in the process of development. Whereas the standard of living is higher in the former, the latter are subject to extreme poverty. The solidarity which binds all men together as members of a common family makes it impossible for wealthy nations to look with indifference upon the hunger, misery and poverty of other nations whose citizens are unable to enjoy

even elementary human rights. The nations of the world are becoming more and more dependent on one another, but even so it will not be possible to preserve a lasting peace so long as these glaring economic and social inequalities persist.

The pope lists many ways in which help can and should be given. Private and public enterprise must play their part, positively, in helping developing nations. He stresses the need for cooperation between the peoples of the world in doing this and he takes the unusual step of singling out in the Encyclical a public body for special praise for its work in helping the lesser-developed countries of the world, namely the Food and Agriculture Organization of United Nations.

Balanced development necessary

The pope praises those nations which enjoy a high degree of economic wealth and who help the under-developed nations to raise their own standards of living. While he realizes, in common with all agricultural economists, that the huge farm surpluses in some of the more prosperous countries cannot, even if the problems of distributing such immense amounts were solved, contribute permanently to raising the standards of living in the under-developed countries, he nevertheless stresses the need to use such surpluses for emergency aid because the squandering of goods offering people a chance of survival is against equity and kindness. As I write at the end of August 1962, the F.A.O. and United Nations have jointly organized a Conference to arrange that food surpluses may be put into a kind of World Food Bank where they would be available for emergency famine aid, for social work in the under-developed countries, such as school meals for children, and for helping on the economic programme of a country where industrial works might provide additional wage earners whose demand for food from the internal market could easily cause inflationary rises in prices.

The only permanent remedy, he says, for the primitive and undeveloped state of a nation's economy is to make use of every possible means of providing its own citizens with the scientific, technical and professional training that they need, and to put at their disposal the necessary capital for speeding up their economic development with the help of modern methods.

We are aware how deeply the public conscience has been affected in recent years by the urgent need of supporting the economic development and social progress of these countries which are still struggling against poverty and economic disabilities. . . . It is a magnificent work that they are doing and we are most happy to take this occasion of giving it the praise it deserves. It is work however, which needs to be increased and we hope that the years ahead will see the wealthy nations making even greater efforts for the scientific, technical and economic advancement of those political communities in which development is still only in its initial stages.

The declaring of a "Development Decade" by the United Nations is in keeping with this plea of the pope. The pope warns against allowing the newly developed communities to repeat the errors of the past. In this he is echoing the words of Pius XII:

As to the countries where industrialism begins today to be envisaged, we can only lend the weight of ecclesiastical authority to sparing populations, which have lived until now in a patriarchal or feudal régime and, above all, in diverse groups, the repetition of the grievous omissions of economic liberalism in the last century. Even with regard to this new industrialization the question still remains: does it or does it not contribute to the reintegration and security of a healthy productivity in the national economy? Or alternatively, does it only multiply still further the number of industries always at the mercy of recurring crises? And then, where the investment of capital is guided only by the desire for short-lived advantages and where there is an empty pride in national prestige, what care will be taken to consolidate and develop the home market, made productive by reason of the importance of the population and the multiplicity of its needs.

He stresses that every sector of the economy, agriculture, industry and public services must progress evenly and simultaneously to ensure that social progress keeps pace with economic progress. In calling for foreign aid to help the more equitable distribution of this world's goods, the pope stresses that such technical and financial aid should be offered with political disinterestedness to allow developing countries an advancement in economic and political life in keeping with their own individuality. In helping these backward nations, therefore, the more advanced communities must recognize and respect this individuality. They must beware of making the assistance they give an excuse for forcing these people into their own national mould.

The Christian commitment to this world

Pope John XXIII makes it clear from the very fact that he has written such a down-to-earth Encyclical, going into the details of economic and social life, that such concern is part of the mission of the Church and that it is rightly part of the action of individual Catholics. There has been sometimes a tendency in some quarters in the past to regard social and economic matters as somehow out of keeping with the spiritual work of the Church or the spiritual life of the individual. Nicholas Berdyaev has a passage in his *The Fate of Man in the Modern World* which describes this:

> Christian piety has all too often seemed to be a withdrawal from the world and from men, a sort of transcendent egoism, the unwillingness to share the suffering of the world and man. It was not sufficiently infused with Christian love and mercy. It lacked human warmth and the world has risen in protest against this form of piety as a refined form of egoism, as indifference to the world's sorrow. Against this protest only reborn piety can stand; care for the life of another, even material bodily care, is spiritual in essence; bread for myself is a material question, bread for my neighbour is a spiritual question.

Pius XII had been conscious of this danger and his words are a warning to people that they must not be so heavenly minded that they were no earthly good. He showed how the whole history of the Church was full of deeds of Christian charity at a very practical level. He said:

> Do not let yourselves be misled by the manufacturers of errors and unhealthy theories . . . currents of thought which hold that since redemption belongs to the sphere of supernatural grace and is therefore exclusively the work of God, there is no need for us to cooperate on earth. . . . As if the first efficacy of grace were not to cooperate with our sincere efforts to fulfil every day the commandments of God, as individuals and members of society; as if, for the last two thousand years, there has not lived in the Church the sense of the collective responsibility of all for all; so that souls were moved and are moved to heroic charity: the souls of the monks who cultivated the land, those who freed the slaves, those who heal the sick, those who spread the faith, civilization and sciences to all ages and to all peoples, to create social conditions which are alone capable of making possible and feasible for all a life worthy of a man and of a Christian.

Pope John XXIII has similar injunctions and warnings for Catholics who fear that too much immersion in everyday life may hamper their own spiritual development or perfection. He says, towards the end of the Encyclical, speaking about the Christian's work in the world:

> We have only been able to touch lightly upon this matter. But our sons, the laity especially, must not suppose that they would be acting prudently to lessen their personal Christian commitment in this passing world. On the contrary we insist that they must intensify it and increase it continually. In his solemn prayer for the Church's unity, Christ our Lord did not ask his Father to remove his disciples from the world: "I pray not that thou shouldst take them out of the world, but that thou shouldst keep them from evil."
>
> Let no man therefore imagine that a life of activity in the world is incompatible with spiritual perfection. The two can very well be harmonized. It is a gross error to suppose that a man cannot perfect himself except by putting aside all temporal activity on the plea that such activity will inevitably lead him to compromise his personal dignity as a human being and as a Christian.
>
> That a man should develop and perfect himself through his

daily work—that in most cases is of a temporal character—is perfectly in keeping with the plan of divine Providence. The Church today is faced with an immense task: to humanize and Christianize this modern civilization of ours. Its continual development and indeed its very survival demand and insist that the Church do her part in the world. That is why, as we said before, she claims the cooperation of her laity. In conducting their human affairs to the best of their ability, they must recognize that they are doing a service to humanity, in intimate union with God through Christ and to God's greater glory. And St Paul insisted: "Whether you eat or drink or whatever else you do, do all for the glory of God." "All whatsoever you do in word or in work, do all in the name of the Lord Jesus Christ, giving thanks to God and the Father by him."

SOME RESULTS OF MATER ET MAGISTRA

The above sketch of the main ideas in *Mater et Magistra*, as far as they affect the developing countries, shows that the Church has a sound social doctrine which can be applied, and if it were applied, would supply the solution to the problems of the developing countries. The Encyclical is noteworthy because, unlike many Encyclicals, there is no denunciation, little harsh condemnation of errors. Indeed the only harsh condemnation is reserved for the action of those who, in their desire to bring economic aid, neglect or even destroy spiritual values, as if the provision of bread alone were sufficient. In the following chapter, we shall deal with the combination of economic aid and Christian humanism which the pope stresses so much in the Encyclical.

The tremendous value of the Encyclical is that it puts all the weight of the pope's authority behind all those who have been devotedly striving to help the less fortunate countries. It will arouse the interest and action of those Catholics who so far have remained aloof, for they will see that they cannot remain loyal Catholics and be indifferent to the pope's words. Indeed, this work of stimulating action has begun already, for this Encyclical is a call to action not to theorizing.

South America

The Fifth International Rural Life Congress held in Autumn 1961 near Caracas in Venezuela on the initiative of Mgr L. Ligutti (the devoted apostle of Rural Life Improvement who is Permanent Observer of the Holy See at the Food and Agriculture Organization) had for its title *Mater et Magistra.*

Lectures and discussions throughout the congress were linked to the new social Encyclical. Top statesmen from Latin American countries were speakers and delegates were from almost every Latin American country. The President of Venezuela, President Betancourt, was the principal speaker at the closing session.

It was made abundantly clear that the Encyclical had already had an immense impact on the thinking of Catholics in the social apostolate in Latin America. It is held by them as providing just what is needed for their socially and economically backward countries. The wonderful section on agriculture has a very great relevance to South America, since such a large proportion of the people of these developing countries depend on agriculture.

The bishops present took the opportunity of stating: "There is not one bishop in the whole of South America who does not stand four-square behind land reform." Since then, sensational and revolutionary action has shown that they were not paying lip service to these principles. A nation-wide agrarian reform project of the Catholic Church in Chile was announced several months after the congress (in December, 1961) with a twofold object: Better use of the land for the common good, and a greater participation by the rural working families in the ownership and income from the land.

The bishops in every diocese have given away land belonging to the Church at considerable sacrifice, for, as they pointed out in a joint pastoral in March, 1962: "The income from these lands has been used entirely to maintain the charitable, educational and welfare work of the Church." Bishop Errazuriz of Talca, Chile, has given 8,600 acres of Church land to landless Chilean farm-hands making the first settlement erected on former Church property. Each settler family gets 37 acres of irrigated land. The rest of the land, including pasturage, will be held in common. The entire land holding of the Church in Chile is estimated at 14,800 acres.

Other similar gestures are reported from South America. For example, a bishop in Colombia gave up his own large house for social work and has gone to live in a much smaller one. The President of Venezuela officially declared that the Encyclical "will be our programme".

One practical outcome was the bringing into existence of a federation of Venezuelan Cooperatives and Credit Unions. This work has received an enormous fillip from the encouragement given to such forms of combination by *Mater et Magistra*.

A new Catholic college is to be established in Costa Rica, modelled on the lines of the famous St Francis Xavier's Extension Department, the Coady International Institute of Antigonish, Nova Scotia, for the purpose of teaching people all over Latin America how to establish Credit Unions and Cooperatives.

Senhor Joao de Souza, a Brazilian economist, said that 75 per cent of Latin America's 200 million people live on the land. A mere 6 per cent of the landowners own 70 per cent of the tillable land. Over three-quarters of the people own 5 to 10 per cent of the land in use. Between 30 and 40 per cent exist without "the basic essentials of life". President Betancourt said that while his country had the highest *per capita* income on paper in Latin America (due to the oil companies), Venezuelan families in their hundreds of thousands live "without medical aid, without schools, without churches, on the margin of the national life".

In Franco's Spain the Encyclical has also had a powerful effect. In the summer of 1962 General Franco announced that the Encyclical would be taken as the model for the social policies of his government and to prove that this was no mere window-dressing, he has reorganized his Cabinet and taken into it ministers, including two *Opus Dei* men, who are known for their interest in social reform on the lines of the social teaching of the Church; and improvements have already been made.

It is interesting to note that the pope nowhere attacks Communism or suggests that Catholics should engage in social and economic improvement in less developed countries as a means of combating the efforts of Communism. This was no doubt because the pope wanted it to be abundantly clear that the thinking of the Church is not negative. He states what the Church is for; not what she is against. In fact, of course, if the teaching of the Church, as outlined in the Encyclical, were to be put into practice in the under-developed countries, there would be no need, as I have already suggested, to attack Communism which thrives on land hunger, proletarian injustice and frustrated legitimate nationalism. Every child who dies of starvation, it has been said, is an argument for Communism. A concerted attack on world hunger and world poverty which the Encyclical should lead to, would remove the conditions on which Communism thrives. It could not do so immediately because the problem is too great, but if it were seen everywhere that the Church and those politicians and governments who profess to take their inspiration from the Church, who profess to be Christian governments, were seen to be committed to the attack on world poverty in a genuine and wholehearted way, this would be sufficient of itself to make men see that the Church has the answers which satisfy man's material needs as well as his spiritual aspirations and that Communism has not got all the answers; in fact, that its answers are partial and unsatisfying ones.

CHAPTER VII

ECONOMICS AND
CHRISTIAN HUMANISM

From all that has gone before it is clear that poverty could be wiped off the face of the earth in this century, and it is our duty to see to it by hard work and ingenuity that it is. In face of the great problems, heart-rending as they are, we must not panic. Poverty must be wiped out, without wiping out the human values which are what really give men human dignity. We must not submit to an existential morality which would be prepared to use any means, moral or immoral, to achieve this so laudable end.

THE IMPORTANCE OF HUMAN VALUES

Economic means not enough

We must have the courage to face the fact that the poverty and other evils which afflict the less-favoured half of the world did not grow overnight nor will they be banished overnight. Over-rapid generalization and excessive simplification must be avoided at all costs. Under-development is not a homogeneous phenomenon that can be abstracted from its historical and geographical setting so as to serve as a model case, reduced to a few variants. It is a changing human situation with all that that implies, involving trial and error, patience and perseverance, adaptability on the part of those who are to help, and above all, respect for human beings as individuals. There is too great a tendency in present writing on the subject to consider economic development as an end in itself. It is but a means, in fact, though no doubt a very important one, towards the essential objective for every human being, a standard of living worthy of his spiritual potential. The necessity of providing aid has a moral aspect and an economic aspect; social justice, as we have seen, imposes on rich countries a moral obligation which implies an appeal to charity and this needs to be put into practice in the shape of effective, equitable and generous international aid. The economic aid should essentially be a cooperative undertaking between men and men; so it must not be, on any terms, regarded as a mere diffusion of highly capitalistic production methods, of a kind unlikely to suit many countries whose essential problem is rather to get more productive work out of a numerous and relatively cheap labour force. Wrong ideas in this sphere are at the root of grave errors such as the installation of certain huge industrial undertakings with no economic justification and also a prevalent lack of interest in agriculture. Economic aid should not be considered as a means of exporting to under-developed countries the economic structures of Western capital whether good or bad. It has got to be a sharing of the economic and technical progress of the developed countries with the rest of the world on terms and by means adapted to the requirements and mentality of these countries. Thus conceived, economic aid will constitute not only relief, necessarily of a restricted and temporary nature, to the burden that the under-developed countries have to bear; it will also have a stimulating effect, an educative one, enabling those countries to pass on from their present under-developed situations, which is due to a special range of circumstances, to the phase of "self-sustaining growth".[1]

But the very position of economic superiority which the West represents to the developing countries is inclined to give

[1] Cf. Mertens de Wilmars, *loc. cit.*

them an undue respect for all that these countries stand for. That is why their responsibility, as Pope John XXIII has pointed out, is so great and he warns that they must not exploit this advantage to neglect the true hierarchy of values. Scientific and technical progress, he says, economic development and the betterment of living conditions, are certainly valuable elements in a civilization. But we must realize that they are essentially instrumental in character, they are not supreme values in themselves. The pope stresses this in *Mater et Magistra*:

It pains us therefore to observe complete indifference to the true hierarchy of values shown by so many people in the economically developed countries. Spiritual values are ignored, forgotten or denied, while the progress of science technology and economics is pursued for its own sake, as though material well being were the be-all and end-all of life. This attitude is contagious, especially when it affects the work that is being done for the under-developed countries which have often preserved in their ancient traditions an acute and vital awareness of the more important human values. To attempt to undermine this national integrity is essentially immoral. It must be respected and as far as possible clarified and developed, so that it may remain what it is: a foundation of true civilization.

And in another place the pope comes back to this hierarchy of values:

Certainly the Church teaches—and has always taught—that scientific and technical progress and the resultant material well-being are good things and mark an important phase in human civilization. But the Church teaches, too, that goods of this kind must be valued according to their true nature: as instruments used by man for the better attainment of his end. They help to make him a better man both in the natural and supernatural orders. These warning words of the divine Master ever sound in men's ears: "For what does it profit a man if he gains the whole world and suffer the loss of his own soul; for what exchange shall a man give for his soul?"

THE RÔLE OF CHRISTIAN LOVE

The duty of giving economic aid, therefore, implies the duty of seeing that this is given in no soulless spirit. Brash materialism of a capitalist nature is almost as damaging as, and it is more subtle than, the more obvious materialism of Communist countries with their open avowal of the aim of "a material paradise on earth", of the "fact" that material things are the only things that count. The Western nations have a Christian heritage and they need to show the influence of that heritage in their dealings with the countries of the East especially, and with all the developing countries. Their aid must be given in a spirit of justice and charity, in true partnership with the developing countries, so that all trace of exploitation, of paternalism, of condescending financial aid with strings, of a new imperialism, will be absent. With Christian love as a motive force, these evils will be avoided and in their place will come a genuine co-operation between the developed and the developing nations of the world. This will lead to a balanced growth which will give full scope to their spiritual and cultural heritage and help them to avoid undue and crippling rivalry, xenophobic nationalism and the evils of waste and extravagance.

As Bishop Fulton Sheen has pointed out, we should avoid trying to win people to our orbit by economic means alone. To do this would be to put ourselves on exactly the same basis as the Soviets, namely materialism. Denying it in theory, but affirming it in practice, we would thereby assume the basic Marxist principle of the exclusively materialistic character of human life and the principle of the economic determination of history. And what would be tragic is that we would be doing it to peoples who themselves refuse to accept the primacy of the economic.

Our assistance must be in keeping with our belief in God, in the dignity of the human person and the value of individual freedom of conscience, in the principle that the state exists for man, not man for the state.

It must, as I have said, be based on real love, Christian love. The inspired words of St Paul on the excellence of charity describe the spirit in which we should approach this partnership.

This need not be feared as unrealistic, as too "pious" an attitude to the economic realities of aid or as too exclusive a shutting out of those who do not share our Catholic or Christian faith. We will find many allies in the West among those who do not openly profess any religion, or even belief in God. In basing the fundamental solution of these world problems on Christian love, regarding the nations as members of one human family helping each other in the give and take of family life, one might indeed be regarded by some as naïve and idealistic. That is either because they have not realized the value of these ideas or are ashamed to put them forward. Yet a philosopher so far removed from the Catholic viewpoint as Bertrand Russell has said the same thing: "The root of the matter, if we want a stable world, is a very simple and old-fashioned thing, a thing so simple that I am almost ashamed to mention it for fear of the derisive smile with which cynics will greet my words. The thing I mean is love, Christian love, or compassion."

Let us examine the actual situation and see what a transformation an attitude of Christian love would bring about, is already bringing about.

AID MUST BE IN A SPIRIT OF DISINTERESTED PARTNERSHIP

Pierre Moussa has said that the greatest threat of World War III comes from the ambition, the degradation and poverty of the under-developed countries. These hungry millions, these aspiring but frustrated nations, represent an enormous potential of explosive material. Before their eyes, unconsciously often, sometimes even unwillingly, is flaunted Western wealth. They need help but it is always difficult to ask for it, doubly so when a country is recently free and is wishing to prove its independence without the means to do so. They have been helped at times in the past, in a spirit of patronage, or self-interest, sometimes it has been made clear to them that they are pawns in a political game, they are expected to fit into the political and military framework of their sponsor out of gratitude for his gifts. This kind of thing breeds resentment; it can drive a country "out of cussedness" into an opposite course, it can make a country treat its benefactors with arrogance, even while it is dependent on their largesse.

This complacency and selfishness on the part of donor nations, which poorer nations are inclined to see even when it is not there, cannot exist where there is true love, for love means considering the other, his feelings, his interests, as much as oneself.

There are numbers of examples of lavish assistance given in the last decade bringing enmity and jealousy rather than gratitude, on account of the spirit in which it was given. The problem of giving aid, in forms of investment, loans, gifts, or technical assistance, as we have seen, is an urgent one: it is also a delicate one.

The giving of aid cannot be regarded as a competition be-tween great powers: who can give the most aid or get the biggest propaganda or political advantage out of it. It is too important: it concerns human beings too much to be made a gambit of the Cold War. Aid must be of a nature not to injure the recipients. It should unite economics and Christian human-ism, Christian concern for human beings. Alone economic aid is sometimes powerless or even harmful before the magnitude and nature of our problem. Perhaps in no other field is the saying of St Augustine so true: "Love without knowledge goes astray, knowledge without love leads to pride, only love with knowledge is constructive."

The work of Père Lebret

Père L. J. Lebret, O.P., has perhaps best expressed this idea of combining economics and true human values. His basic contention is that the poverty of the masses exists because of the lack of humanity in an economy based solely on profit, the anarchy of the liberal economy, and that there is the urgent necessity to discover beyond Marxism and capitalism an economic system that would be human, that it is possible to find men who are technicians and thoroughly disinterested to get structures changed to the profit of all people. After a long period of applying these ideas in France in collaboration with prominent men of good will, putting human dignity and the common good foremost in his theorizing and practical work, Père Lebret, who is now recognized as an economist of international stature, shown by his position as advisor to the governments of Senegal and the Lebanon, has applied his "Economie et Humanisme" movement to the under-developed countries in the last decade.

PRINCIPLES OF DEVELOPMENT AND CIVILIZATION

In 1958, a Training Institute was established in Paris under the presidency of Robert Buron, Minister of Transport and Public Works. This Institute is called I.R.F.E.D.[2]—The International Training and Research Centre for Development— with a very high-class periodical *Développement et Civilisations*. The main characteristics of I.R.F.E.D. may be summed up in the words of Madeleine Trebous, editor of the periodical:

a. Development ought to be overall and evenly balanced, that is to say, it should meet all the needs of all the people and coordinate all steps being taken by the state and its various services and by private bodies.

b. For I.R.F.E.D., development means "*the series of transformations for a social population, together with all groups of human beings who are within it, from a less human standard of life to a more human, at the quickest speed possible, at the lowest cost possible, taking into account the solidarity between all sections of population and international solidarity*" (L. J. Lebret).

[2] "Institut International de Recherche et de Formation en vue du Developpement Harmonisé."

c. I.R.F.E.D. holds that economic systems for so-called developed countries are not to be applied uncritically to newly developing countries. New ways must be found.

d. I.R.F.E.D. insists more and more on the necessity to integrate various sciences in order to achieve a really human development, involving economic, medical welfare, cultural, educational, moral, civic, rural development.

e. I.R.F.E.D. endeavours to find out and spread methods that may be applied to developments that are complex, of long-term character and broad scope, so that the setting up of administrative structures is made easy.

f. I.R.F.E.D. holds also that development ought to be self-generating, that is to say, progress in any field must produce enough material and human possibilities for the new step to be taken.

g. Also development should be continuous: it is not made up of one single isolated action, taken once and for all, but is considered in its long-term effects and reorientated according to new needs, new evolutions, events, obstacles or new possibilities.

h. In one word, I.R.F.E.D. aims at creating a new civilization or new civilizations, where each human being would have enough to live decently and to progress in human value.

I.R.F.E.D. is a private research international institute, doing at the same time practical work in connection with other organizations, and training every year about eighty young economists, architects, doctors, sociologists, agronomists, social welfare officers, mathematicians, etc from many countries (twenty-five in 1961) in these methods of development in newly developing countries.

The aims of this private endeavour which is backed by many outstanding public men seem to be an excellent fulfilment of the ideals and concrete suggestions of *Mater et Magistra*. They sum up what has been the theme running through this book, what I would regard as the golden thread of Catholic thought on the problems of under-development, expressing the urgency of the need of raising the living standards of the people of the under-developed world which are out of keeping with the human dignity of human beings by overall development not merely economic improvement. This would restore and enhance human dignity which neither secularized materialism nor dehumanized Marxism can hope to do, because they neglect the spiritual element in man, an essential part of his nature.

WORLD JUSTICE

The international situation now imposes on Catholics an obligation to work for a code of international social justice in line with the principles of the natural law, of which the Church is the guardian and interpreter, and at the same time in harmony with the facts of our twentieth-century world.

In this connection, the Research Centre for International Social Justice recently founded in Louvain aims to meet the need, as it should be met, at the highest level. It seeks, by means of its high-class periodical *World Justice*, to mobilize the best theologians, moralists and social scientists of the day to develop these principles to guide the statesmen of the world. But not only these; to be of practical value, the cooperation of the world's best specialists in economics, agriculture, international law, history, technology and related sciences is being sought and some outstanding contributions have already been made since the Centre's foundation in 1959.

There is no doubt that the ideals behind the United Nations Charter and the Agencies such as F.A.O., W.H.O., U.N.E.S.C.O., and other organizations are largely in keeping with these Catholic social principles. For example, article 22 of the United Nations Declaration of Human Rights sums this up: "Everyone, as a member of society, has the right to social security and, in accordance with the organization and resources of each state, of the economic, social and cultural rights indispensable for his dignity and the free development of his personality."

This is true in spite of the fact that in working out day-to-day policies of these U.N. Agencies, of course, there are elements which are not in complete agreement with Catholic ideas. There are also practical reasons why a good proportion of aid should be channelled through them, as we have seen.

Moreover, there is no reason why, with countries with mature and adult statesmen such as India, who can admit with dignity that they *are* poor and do need help and are prepared by self-help and cooperation to work with governments ready to assist them, inter-governmental and bilateral aid should not be as acceptable and sometimes less cumbersome and more effective. The criterion should be what is the most acceptable and most effective way of giving assistance.

Here it may be well to stress the responsibilities of the poorer countries, for assistance to these countries should be based on honesty and truth. It is, as I have stressed, of the greatest importance for the donor countries to avoid condescending charity, to rub in the fact that these countries are poor and that they are rich. Still no good purpose is served by refusing to face the facts of life, to pretend these countries are not poor, to pretend that they are rich enough to afford extravagance or irresponsibility or costly policies not geared to the urgent basic needs of their people.

THE DEMOCRATIC RÔLE OF ORDINARY PEOPLE

Most of this book has been concerned with aid on a large scale; it was impossible to go into overmuch detail: it has been concerned with policies some of which seem to be beyond the range of ordinary people, everyday Catholics, as if they had no part to play.

If we believe at all in democracy, this attitude is false on several grounds. It is possible and necessary for us to influence the actions of our elected leaders and to bring pressure to bear on governments.

Putting it bluntly, if enough ordinary people were educated to the need and urgency of the problem of world poverty, something would be done about it. As it is, governments are not doing enough, though they are often further ahead than their people. Although world poverty is the central problem of our time, it is still not a live issue before electorates. As Catholics we need to be well informed, concerned and committed and join with all others of good will to proclaim "from the housetops", as Pope John XXIII has said, the fact that millions still go hungry, that millions live in grinding poverty and to demand that something be done about it. We are tremendously fortunate in being the heirs of a priceless Faith, one of the decisive formative influences of Western civilization. To bear witness to that Faith we have to apply its principles in everyday life. By these very principles, we know that the present division of the world's wealth is manifestly unjust. Here then is a situation calling for Christian action.

There are a number of ways in which Catholics can help, indeed, are helping. Throughout the world, missionaries in the under-developed countries are combining the work of preaching the Gospel with raising the living standards, the human dignity, of less privileged people. As Pope John XXIII has said in *Mater et Magistra*:

> The Church is by divine right universal. History itself bears this out, for the Church is present everywhere on earth, doing all that she can to embrace all peoples.
>
> Now, in bringing people to Christ, the Church has invariably—both now and in the past—brought them many social and economic advantages. These new converts to Christianity cannot help feeling obliged to improve their own temporal institutions and environment. They do all they can to prevent these institutions from doing violence to human dignity. They encourage whatever is conducive to honesty and virtue, and strive to eliminate every obstacle to the attainment of this aim.
>
> Moreover, in becoming, as it were, the life-blood of these people, the Church is not, nor does she consider herself to be, a foreign body in their midst. Her presence brings about the rebirth, the resurrection, of each individual in Christ; and the man who is reborn and rises again in Christ never feels himself constrained from without. He feels himself free in the very depth of his being, and freely raised up to God. And thus he affirms and develops that side of his nature which is noblest and best.

This work is supported by voluntary contributions, generous but not generous enough. In America a hundred times the amount given to the Society for the Propagation of the Faith is spent on dog food.

CHRISTIAN VOLUNTARY AGENCIES

There are many voluntary agencies working for the relief and betterment of poverty-stricken people throughout the world. These organizations make use of private charity to bring immediate effective relief. Several may be singled out as typical of these organizations: the N.C.W.C. in the United States and the Oxford Famine Relief Fund in England and *Misereor* and *Caritas* on the Continent.

The Relief Services of the National Catholic Welfare Conference (N.C.W.C.) of the American hierarchy have done untold good since the war in administering individual gifts and government aid for the benefit of the under-developed world, especially in times of famine, war and other disasters. This organization has distributed government surpluses and in turn the United States government has enabled it to feed the hungry, clothe the naked and nurse the sick. Bishop Swanstrom of the N.C.W.C. says of this cooperation:

> The efforts of the voluntary agencies have been substantially aided by the United States Government. Substantial quantities of government surplus food have been donated to the voluntary agencies for distribution overseas. In the majority of instances, our government has assumed the cost of the freight, not only of the surplus commodities, but also of relief supplies generated independently by the voluntary agencies. It is for this basic reason that America's voluntary agencies programme reaches more than 60 million needy people overseas.

Voluntary agencies have proved that they can administer overseas relief programmes efficiently and economically. Because of this they are now requesting government aid in the financing of reconstruction projects to supplement present relief programmes.

Bishop Swanstrom underlines the importance of this: "The people of the under-developed countries of the world learn

more about the fundamental differences between the dictator-
ships and Communists and the freedoms of the Western world
through the activities of the voluntary agencies."

The amount of generous aid of all kinds that the American
people and the American government have given since World
War II is unparalleled in history. It has added a new dimension
to Christian charity and helped powerfully to form a climate
favourable to concern for the under-developed countries and
the principle of international social justice and charity by action
and example. There are of course many other American
organizations, inter-denominational or attached to certain
creeds, for relief. N.C.W.C. has been chosen as a typical example of work in this field.

The Relief Fund of the German bishops, *Misereor*, which
receives the Lenten alms of the German Catholics and has
already raised millions of dollars for the poorer countries, is
another example of practical Christian charity, giving direct
help where it is most needed. It gave 100,000 dollars for the
Freedom from Hunger Campaign Fund—the first contribution received—when that was started in 1960. Among many of
its works of charity, it has endowed twenty-three leper settle-
ments throughout the world.

In England the Family Fast Fund, sponsored by the Catholic
Women's League, combined personal sacrifice of a practical
nature, the whole family fasting for one day and giving the
proceeds to the Fund, with help to the needy. This fund
"adopted" the island of Dominica and put at the disposal of
relief and social workers there the money saved by their scheme.
Out of this has grown the Catholic Fund for Overseas Development of the English Hierarchy set up in 1962.

Incidentally, the practical manner in which the Freedom
from Hunger Campaign can be helped by private charity is
illustrated by the way it is already working in England. The
Projects method makes people feel that their money is being
well used and arouses a personal interest in a particular scheme
to help the under-privileged in a particular place. Three small

towns in England, Carlisle, Skipton and Windsor, the first to adopt one of the projects, give an example of how it works. They have undertaken to raise £27,000 over the next three years to help some Indian villages to become self-supporting.

The Oxford Committee for Famine Relief (OXFAM) of England is an internationally known relief agency noted, during its twenty years of collecting and distributing aid, for its uniquely effective, rapid and devoted service to those hit by famine, war, earthquake or other disasters. Although most of its members are Christians and it has a strong religious motivation, it is completely undenominational, helping all regardless of race, creed or politics. Catholics in England have a special interest in it, as they contribute largely to it, and in turn, OXFAM has given generous assistance to Catholic works of charity overseas. It is now extending its scope to include longer-term measures of assistance as well as immediate relief.

The work of these and other voluntary organizations shows that although the problems of under-developed countries—immense as they are—cannot be completely tackled by private charity, very much worth-while help has and can be given by such means.

But the need to awaken the consciences of the peoples of the West is pressing. Ordinary decent people must be made aware of the facts of world poverty. Most of them have not realized that a modern Gospel parable would inexorably cast them for the rôle of Dives. Bishop Fulton Sheen has suggested that we need to justify our wealth by sharing it: "It is their stomachs that are empty: it could be that our hearts are empty. In any case, they could conceivably do without our aid but we cannot continue to be without justice and charity."

And the Abbé Pierre has expressed the same idea with his usual forthrightness: "The real blasphemy is not the despairing curse of the father unable to feed his starving child. It is the indifference of those who could have enabled him to feed it."

ONE WORLD

As World Refugee Year showed—in England the target was surpassed by four times the amount asked for—the best antidote to lack of concern is knowledge. That is why the Freedom from Hunger Campaign is insisting so much on informing and educating people to a realization of the plight of the under-privileged people, rather than on fund-raising. Funds and action will come once people know and reflect that they are their brother's keeper in this world of ours, made one by the marvels of science which enable us to span the globe in days and have news reported and even seen while it is happening.

The idea of mankind as a single family under the Fatherhood of God is so much a foundation of Christian thinking that it is simply taken for granted and not thought about at all. Certainly this idea is not constantly studied and acted upon in the second half of the twentieth century when the unity of mankind is stressed by the physical and economic unity which barriers of geographical ignorance or poor communications no longer impede. Today, we can see on our television or cinema screens the misery of famine, the destitution of refugees, the diseases of the underfed. As Pope John has said in a passage already quoted: "Nobody can offer the excuse in a world where distances count for nothing, that he is unaware of the needs of his far-away brother or that it is not his job to help him."

That consciences are stirring on national and individual levels we have already seen. But no one can pretend that the schemes for aid and technical assistance are worthy of the West or are proportionate to the problems.

NEED FOR THE WEST TO COMPLETE THE REVOLUTION IT HAS BEGUN

Deliberately, I have avoided in this book founding our duty of giving aid on restitution for past wrongs or as a payment owed by the colonizing powers for former exploitation. It would be too difficult to get an agreed basis on this and, in any case, it would only stir up old grievances best forgotten and expiated in part at least by enlightened colonial policies since World War II. I have preferred to base the duty of aid on the positive principles of international social justice.

Nevertheless, there is one aspect of the historical relationship between developed and under-developed countries which should not be ignored. By its skills and knowledge, the West has revolutionized the world. The colonial powers especially have transformed whole sectors of the lives of the more backward countries. They have helped to precipitate these peoples, mostly ill prepared, into the progress of modern civilization. The very population explosion is mainly due to the triumphs of Western medicine and hygiene. The crisis it has caused is due mainly to the fact that agriculture has not kept pace with medicine, and industrial and scientific advancement have not partnered medical achievements. Barbara Ward, in *The Rich Nations and Poor Nations* (p. 129), as some profound reflections on why this should be so. She detects a lack of concern, a complacency, too unthinking to be described as "callous" about the revolutions, in our whole world, by the application of technology and capital, which were launched by the North Atlantic nations:

> The changes have been unleashed on mankind. Blindly, blunderingly, with immense impact and immense confusion, they are remaking the face of the earth. But can one say that the Western powers follow their course with any intimate concern? Do they see them as direct projections of the Western way of life or accept responsibility for the fact that it was the Western colonial system that chiefly set in motion the present world-wide movement of revolutionary change?
>
> I wonder why this is. After all, is it not strange to care so little for what we have launched; to lose interest in our inventions just when they are beginning to have their maximum impact?

Miss Ward shows that, while at times this Micawberish attitude may have worked, we are definitely not living in those times now, and that now it is not the Micawbers but those who will and want and work who are more likely to see their visions realized. She goes on:

> It is therefore a disturbing reflection that in our own day the amount of effort, interest, preparation, and sheer slogging hard work which the Communists tend to put into the task of building their version of world order very greatly exceeds what we are ready to do or the sacrifices we are prepared to make. Even more obviously, their vision of a world brotherhood made one by Communism, outstrips the scale of our imagination. The West thinks only marginally in terms of the whole world, the whole family of man. Each group tends to concentrate on its own parochial interests. There is apparently no energy comparable to the worldwide ambitions that set the Communists to work from one end of our planet to the other.

What we need as Catholics, as Christians, as humanitarians, is the perfectly realizable vision of a world freed from want by the partnership of rich and poor. We want an unhesitating acquiesence in the principles of international justice, so much saner and coherent and humane and attractive than the half-baked theory based on a false reading of economic history and erroneous prognostications for the future which, combined with messianic zeal appealing however deceptively against human want and injustice, and an iron discipline, has put nearly one-third of the world under a godless tyranny. We have to be as foresighted, as determined, as ready to work, and go on working, as are our busy Communist comrades.

We have the resources, we have the ideals, we have the principles. The moral energy will not be lacking, especially in the young, if it is called on for a worth-while crusade, not against Communism, or against any particular manifestation of its evils, but *for* a world fit for all human beings to live in.

There are numbers of Christians whose consciences are shocked by the dreadful weapons which can now destroy man and human civilization. Thus campaigns against nuclear warfare, against the horrors of the H-bomb, are sparked off and sustained by intense moral feeling. But even if such campaigns —apparently as yet the concern of comparatively few—were to be successful, there would still remain the equally explosive situation which world poverty constitutes. To attack world poverty is a positive and constructive thing: the nations might find that when they had defeated it, they had also dispelled the fear of destroying themselves.

A GREAT WORK OF CHRISTIAN UNITY

It is natural and right in a book such as this that the subject should be approached from a Catholic angle: otherwise it would not differ materially from other books on the same subject. Through the book has run the conviction that Catholics have a special duty, a special interest, a special contribution arising from their Faith and their principles.

But this is not an exclusive attitude: it does not exclude partnership with anyone of whatever race, religion, colour or creed, who is eager to rid the world of inhuman conditions. Indeed one of the best fields for the action of Christian unity and newly developing spirit of cooperation is surely here. In attacking world poverty Christians need have no doctrinal differences, no dogmatic scruples. Our Lord's words to all Christians are clear; the conditions for admission to eternal life are too definite to cause even Bible scholars to dispute:

> I was hungry and you gave me food.
> I was thirsty and you gave me drink;
> I was a stranger and you brought me home;
> I was naked and you covered me—
> sick and you cared for me.

SELECT BIBLIOGRAPHY

In this series: CHAMBRE, H., S.J.: *Christianity and Communism*; HOLLIS, Christopher: *The Church and Economics* (U.S.A. edn.: *Christianity and Economics*); MARSHALL, John: *Medicine and Morals.*

BENHAM, F.: *Economic Aid to the Undeveloped Countries*, London and New York, Oxford Univ. Press, 1960.

CALDER, Ritchie: *Commonsense about a Starving World*, London, Gollancz, and New York, Macmillan, 1962.

DROGAT, Noël: *The Challenge of Hunger*, London, Burns and Oates, and Westminster, Md., Newman Press, 1962; *Hunger: Can it be Averted?*, London, British Association, 1961.

FARRIS, Donald: *To Plough with Hope*, London, Gollancz, 1958.

GRIFFITHS, P.: *The Changing Face of Communism*, London, The Bodley Head, and Toronto, British Book Service, 1961.

LESTAPIS, S. de, S.J.: *Family Planning and Modern Problems*, London, Burns and Oates, and New York, Herder, 1961.

MARSHALL, John: *Family Planning: The Catholic View*, Louvain, 1962.

MOUSSA, Pierre: *The Under-Privileged Nations*, London, Sidgwick and Jackson, and Toronto, Ambassador Books, 1962.

PIERRE, Abbé: *Man is Your Brother*, London, Geoffrey Chapman, and Westminster, Md., Newman Press, 1958.

ROSTOW, W. W.: *Stages of Economic Growth*, London and New York, Cambridge Univ. Press, 1960.

SAUVY, Alfred: *Fertility and Survival*, London, Chatto and Windus, and New York, Criterion Books, 1961.

SHONFIELD, Andrew: *The Attack on World Poverty*, London, Chatto and Windus, and New York, Random House, 1960.

SPAULL, Hebe: *The World Unites Against Want*, London, Barrie and Rockliff, 1961.

SUENENS, Cardinal L. J.: *Love and Control*, revised edn., London, Burns and Oates, and Westminster, Md., Newman Press, 1962.

THOMAS, J. L., S.J.: *Marriage and Rhythm*, London, Sands, and Westminster, Md., Newman Press, 1957.

WARD, Barbara: *India and the West*, London, Hamish Hamilton, and Toronto, MacLeod, 1961; *Rich Nations and Poor Nations*, London, Hamish Hamilton, and New York, Norton, 1962.

YATES, P. L.: *So Bold an Aim*, Rome, F.A.O., 1955.

ZIMMERMAN, A., S.V.D.: *The Catholic Viewpoint on Overpopulation*, New York, Doubleday, 1961.

The Twentieth Century Encyclopedia of Catholicism

The number of each volume indicates its place in the over-all series and not the order of publication.

TWENTIETH CENTURY ENCYCLOPEDIA OF CATHOLICISM

All titles are subject to change.